Quilts *by the* Calendar

LEISURE ARTS PRESENTS
The Best of Fons & Porter's
For the Love of Quilting

Fill the year — and your home — with the fruits of your favorite pastime by piecing these 12 outstanding quilts! Each month's quilt echoes the beauty of the season. From a breathtaking January snowfall to festive Christmas stars, this impressive lineup of patchwork projects is certain to please. We've included a variety of styles and sizes — wall hangings, lap quilts, and bed quilts. So, gather your fabric and get ready to quilt a year of comfort!

Table of

Contents

January

Blanketed in freshly fallen snow,

this quilted wall hanging will transform a room into a winter wonderland. A large snowflake and a border of snowdrifts create a vision of wintry splendor. Our freezer-paper appliqué method makes cutting the patterns simple.

Winter on the Ohio

Quilt designed and made by Marjorie Mahoney; owned by Liz Porter

Finished Size: 21" x 21"

Materials

3/4 yd white-on-cream print for background and binding
1/2 yd blue variegated print for center snowflake
1/2 yd blue snowflake print for borders
7/8 yd muslin for backing
26" square batting
3/4 yd 18"-wide freezer paper

Cutting

Measurements include 1/4" seam allowance. Follow *Rotary Cutting*, page 71.

From white-on-cream print, cut:

- 1 (22") square for background.
- 5 (2 1/4" x 22") strips for straight-grain binding.

From blue variegated print, cut:

- 1 (13") square for snowflake.

From blue snowflake print, cut:

- 4 (5" x 22") strips for borders.

From muslin, cut:

- 1 (26") square for backing.

Assembly

1. Cut a 13" square of freezer paper. Fold square into fourths and crease to make guidelines. Trace 1/4 snowflake pattern (page 8) onto each section of freezer paper, aligning fold lines, to make complete pattern. Cut out pattern. Press freezer paper onto right side of blue variegated print, centering pattern. Rough-cut fabric around pattern. With freezer paper on top as a guide, appliqué snowflake onto 22" cream background. *(Note: See page 7 for freezer paper appliqué instructions.)*
2. Layer 2 (5" x 22") blue snowflake print strips with right sides facing. Mark 45° angle at end, as shown in *Diagram 1*. Stitch along drawn line. Trim, unfold, and press to reveal mitered corner *(Diagram 2)*. Repeat with remaining 2 strips.
3. To join the 2 sections from Step 2, repeat for remaining corners, as shown in *Diagram 3*. Trim, unfold, and press to reveal border frame *(Diagram 4)*.
4. Cut 4 (3" x 18") strips of freezer paper. Trace border pattern (page 9) onto 2 strips. Reverse pattern and trace onto 2 remaining strips. Cut out pattern strips. Place each strip on right side of border frame, aligning outer edges and mitered seam lines. Press pattern onto fabric. Rough-cut fabric along inner border edge. Center border frame over quilt center, with outer edges aligned, and pin in place. Appliqué border waves in same manner as snowflake.

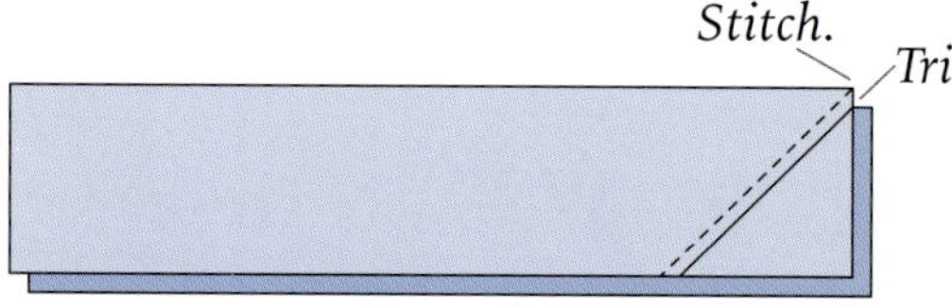

Diagram 1

Diagram 2

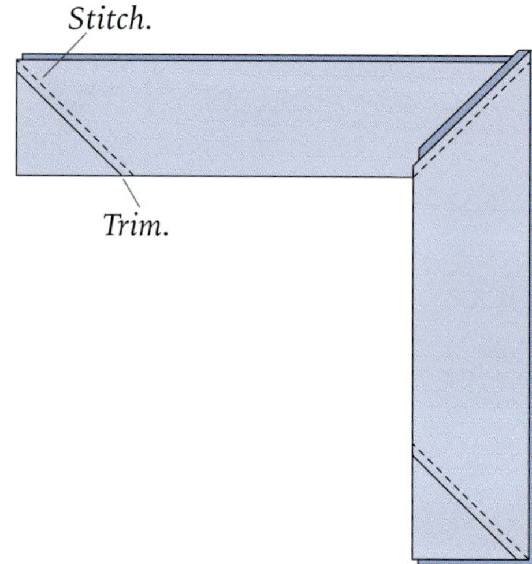

Diagram 3

Diagram 4

Quilting and Finishing

1. Layer backing, batting, and quilt top. Baste. Quilt as desired. Quilt shown was outline-quilted around all appliqué and has an echo-quilted scallop pattern in border.
2. From cream print, make 100" of straight-grain binding. Refer to *Attaching French-Fold Binding with Mitered Corners,* page 79, to add binding to quilt.

Freezer-Paper Appliqué

Try this appliqué method for intricate patterns, like *Winter on the Ohio.*

A

1. Cut a piece of freezer paper the size of your appliqué and fold it in half twice to form equal quadrants. Open it out with coated side down, and trace 1/4 of pattern on 1 section, aligning center and folds.
2. Refold paper. Place pins through pattern to keep folds aligned and cut out. Do not cut along fold lines.
3. Fold square of appliqué fabric in half twice to form equal quadrants and press to form guidelines. Open out freezer-paper pattern and position it on right side of fabric, coated side down, aligning centers and folds. Using a dry iron set for wool, press pattern onto fabric.
4. Position appliqué fabric on top of background fabric, with right sides facing up, and pin.
5. Start at any section of design and carefully cut appliqué fabric approximately 1/8" outside freezer-paper edge for seam allowance *(Photo A).*
6. Clip seam allowance around inside or concave curves, making clips a scant 1/4" apart and approximately 1/8" deep. Use scissor tips to clip straight into seam allowance. Make 1 clip into sharp inside points.
7. Working with point and shank of needle, as well as your fingertips, turn under raw edge of appliqué just ahead of stitching, even with paper edge *(Photo B).* Space stitches no more than 1/8" apart and closer on tight inside corners and curves where there is little or no seam allowance.
8. Remove paper when all edges are appliquéd to background.

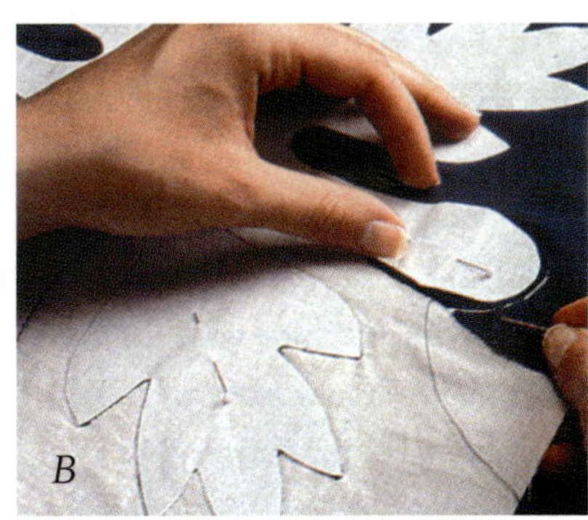
B

1/4 Snowflake Pattern

Border Pattern

February

Love is in the air . . .

especially when this lovely quilt is hanging on your wall! The patchwork of woven hearts reflects how each of us, though different, intertwines with others to forge lasting friendships. Easy enough to complete in a day, this project will make a thoughtful Valentine gift for a special friend.

Woven Hearts

Quilt designed and made by Liz Porter

Finished Size: 22 1/2" x 22 1/2"
Blocks: 6 (5 1/2") Blocks

Materials

1/2 yd of tan-and-red stripe fabric for block backgrounds and borders
1/2 yd of red-and-cream print fabric for borders and binding
9 assorted red print fabric scraps (at least 3" x 4") for hearts
9 assorted cream print fabric scraps (at least 3" x 4") for hearts
3/4 yd heavy-duty paper-backed fusible web
Paper scissors and fabric shears
Rotary cutter, mat, and acrylic ruler
30" square of backing fabric
30" square of precut batting

Cutting

Before cutting pieces, read instructions carefully. Measurements include 1/4" seam allowances. Follow *Rotary Cutting*, page 71.
From tan-and-red stripe fabric, cut:
- 3 (1 1/2"-wide) strips for border strip sets.
- 2 (6"-wide) strips. From these, cut 9 (6") squares.

From red-and-cream fabric, cut:
- 5 (1 1/2"-wide) strips for border strip sets.
- 3 (2"-wide) strips for binding.

Assembly

Making Blocks

1. Trace *Woven Heart Pattern* (page 13) 18 times onto paper side of fusible web, allowing about 1/2" between tracings. Cut out shapes about 1/4" from traced outline.
2. Follow manufacturer's instructions, fuse web to wrong side of 9 red print fabrics and 9 cream fabrics for hearts. Cut out shapes on all drawn lines, including center slits.
3. Choose 1 cream piece and 1 red print piece for each heart. Peel paper backing off each shape. Referring to photo on page 13, weave heart pieces together.
4. Follow manufacturer's instructions to fuse woven hearts to 6" striped background squares. Make total of 9 Woven Heart blocks.
5. Join blocks in 3 horizontal rows of 3 blocks each. Join rows. Press seams in opposite directions from row to row.

Making Pieced Borders

1. Combine red-and-cream print and tan-and-red stripe fabric strips to make 2 strip sets as shown in *Full Strip Set Diagram*. Press seam allowances toward red print.
2. Cut 4 (17"-wide) borders and 4 (1 1/2"-wide) Nine-Patch segments from full strip sets.
3. Cut remaining tan-and-red stripe and red print in half to make 22"-long pieces. Combine strips as shown in *Short Strip Set Diagram* to make 1 short strip set. Press seam allowances toward red strip.
4. From short strip set, cut 8 (1 1/2"-wide) Nine-Patch segments.
5. Referring to *Nine-Patch Diagram*, combine Nine-Patch segments as shown to make 4 Nine-Patch blocks for border corners.
6. Sew 2 borders to opposite sides of quilt top. Press seam allowances toward borders. Sew 1 Nine-Patch block to each end of remaining borders. Sew borders to top and bottom of quilt top.

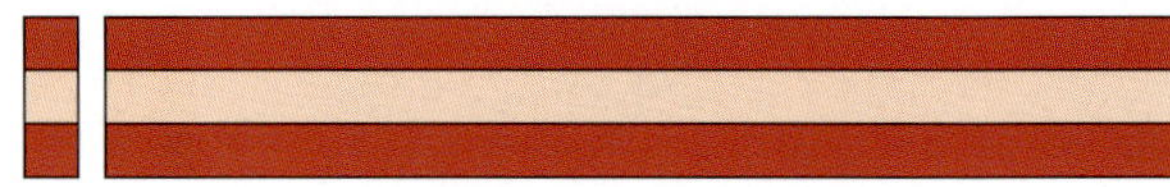

Full Strip Set Diagram

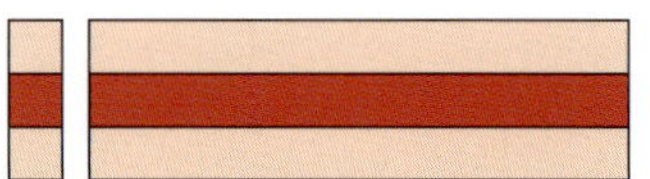

Short Strip Set Diagram

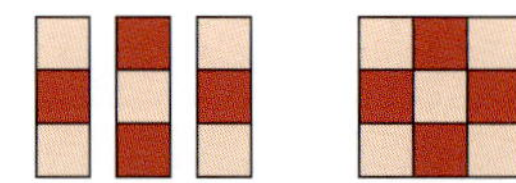

Nine-Patch Diagram

Tip from Liz

I alternated the directions of stripes for my background squares before fusing the hearts in place to enhance the subtle woven effect.

Quilting and Finishing

1. Layer quilt top, batting, and backing; baste.
2. Quilt as desired. Liz machine-quilted 1/4" from hearts and from block seams. She added a row of quilting through red-and-tan fabric in borders and stitched an X through Nine-Patch border squares.
3. Sew binding strips together to make approximately 100" of binding. Follow ***Attaching French-Fold Binding with Mitered Corners,*** page 79, to add binding to wall quilt. If desired, stitch hanging sleeve to quilt back.

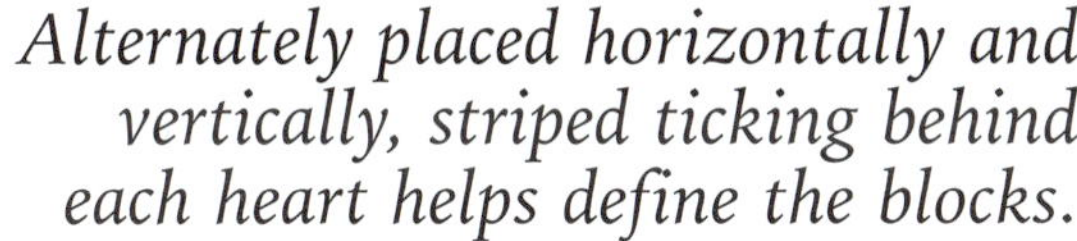

Alternately placed horizontally and vertically, striped ticking behind each heart helps define the blocks.

ADDING A HANGING SLEEVE

Attaching a hanging sleeve to the back of your wall hanging or quilt before the binding is added will allow you to use a dowel rod or wooden slat to display your completed project on a wall.

1. Measure the width of the wall hanging and subtract 1". Cut a piece of fabric 7"w by the determined measurement.
2. Press short edges of fabric piece 1/4" to wrong side twice; machine stitch in place.
3. Matching wrong sides, fold piece in half lengthwise to form a tube.
4. Matching raw edges, baste hanging sleeve to center top edge on back of quilt.
5. Bind quilt as indicated in project instructions, treating the hanging sleeve as part of the backing.
6. Blindstitch bottom of hanging sleeve in place, taking care not to stitch through to front of quilt.
7. Insert rod or slat into hanging sleeve.

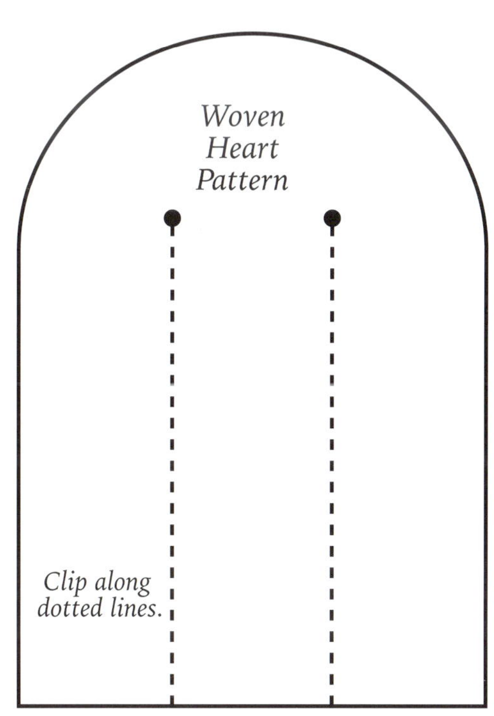

March

Irish eyes won't be the only *ones smiling at this fresh-as-spring quilt! Two traditional quilt blocks — Milky Way and Shoo-Fly — are pieced in green and cream prints to form a quilt that echoes the breathtaking beauty of a field of clover. If you collect fat quarters in a favorite color, use them to assemble your own bonny blanket.*

Scraps of Green

Quilt by Lynn Witzenburg

Finished Size: 87" x 105"
Blocks: 40 (9") Milky Way Blocks and 40 (9") Shoo-Fly Blocks

Materials

40 fat eighths* assorted green prints for blocks
34 fat quarters** assorted light and medium cream prints for background
3/4 yd cream print for border
1 1/4 yds green print for border
3/4 yd dark green print for binding
8 1/4 yds fabric for backing
Queen-size batting
Rotary cutter, cutting mat, and acrylic ruler
* Fat eighth = 9" x 22"
** Fat quarter = 18" x 22"

Cutting

Measurements include 1/4" seam allowances. Follow *Rotary Cutting,* page 71.

From each green fat eighth, cut:
- 3 (2" x 9") strips across 9" width for green/cream strip sets.
- 4 (3 7/8") squares. Cut squares in half diagonally to make 8 B triangles.
- 2 (3 1/2") A squares.
- From green scraps, cut 4 (2") squares for cream border corners.

From each light or medium cream fat quarter, cut:
- 3 (2" x 22") strips for cream strip sets.
- 1 (3 7/8") strip. Cut strip into 5 (3 7/8") squares. Cut squares in half diagonally to make 10 B triangles. You will have 20 extra.
- 3 (2" x 9") strips for green/cream strip sets.

From cream print, cut:
- 9 (2"-wide) strips. Piece to make 2 (2" x 96 1/2") side borders and 2 (2" x 78 1/2") top and bottom borders.

From green print, cut:
- 11 (3 1/2"-wide) strips. Piece to make 2 (3 1/2" x 90") strips and 2 (3 1/2" x 108") strips for outer borders.

From dark green print, cut:
- 10 (2 1/4"-wide) strips for binding.

Milky Way Block Assembly

1. Join 1 (2" x 9") cream strip to 1 green strip to make a strip set. Repeat to make 100 strip sets.
2. Cut 392 (2"-wide) segments from strip sets.
3. Join segments as shown in *Four-Patch Unit Assembly Diagram* to make Four-Patch unit. Make 196 green/cream Four-Patch units.
4. Choose 1 A square, 4 matching green B triangles, and 4 assorted cream B triangles. Join 1 green B and 1 cream B as shown in *Half-Square Triangle Unit Assembly Diagram* to make 1 half-square triangle unit. Make 4 half-square triangle units.
5. Lay out A square, half-square triangle units, and 4 Four-Patch units as shown in *Milky Way Block Assembly Diagram.* Join into rows; join rows to complete 1 block.
6. Make 40 Milky Way blocks.

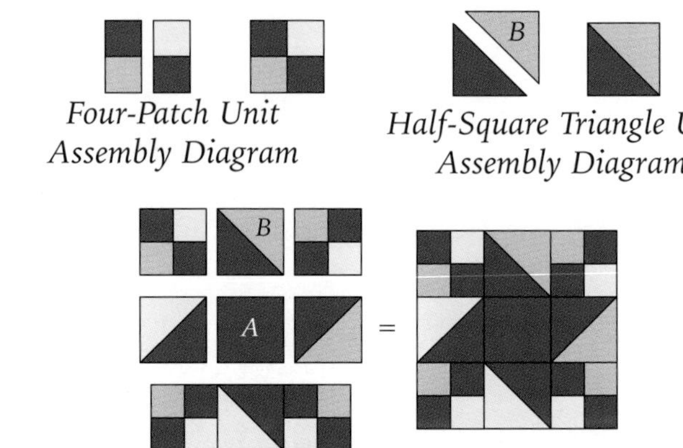

Four-Patch Unit Assembly Diagram

Half-Square Triangle Unit Assembly Diagram

Milky Way Block Assembly Diagram

Shoo-Fly Block Assembly

1. Join 2 (2" x 22") different cream strips to make a strip set. Make 48 strip sets.
2. Cut a total of 472 (2"-wide) segments from strip sets.
3. Join pairs of segments to make 236 cream Four-Patch Units.
4. Choose 1 A square, 4 matching green B triangles, and 4 assorted cream B triangles. Join 1 green B and 1 cream B to make 1 half-square triangle unit. Make 4 half-square triangle units.
5. Lay out A square, half-square triangle units, and Four-Patch units as shown in *Shoo-Fly Block Assembly Diagram.* Join into rows; join rows to complete 1 Shoo-Fly block.
6. Make 40 Shoo-Fly blocks.

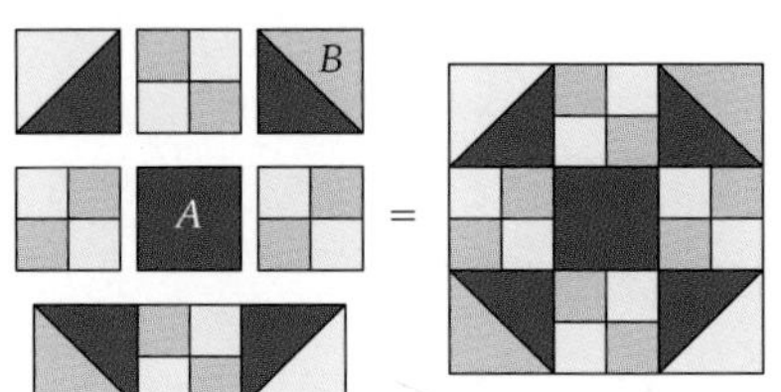

Shoo-Fly Block Assembly Diagram

Border Unit Assembly

1. Join 3 cream Four-Patch units into 1 border unit as shown in *Cream Border Unit Diagram.* Make 18 cream border units.
2. Join 2 green and 1 cream Four-Patch units into 1 green border unit as shown in *Green Border Unit Diagram.* Make 14 green border units.
3. Join 2 cream and 1 green Four-Patch units into 1 corner unit. Make 4 corner units, orienting 2 of each as shown in *Corner Border Unit Diagrams.*
4. Remaining green Four-Patch units are border corners.

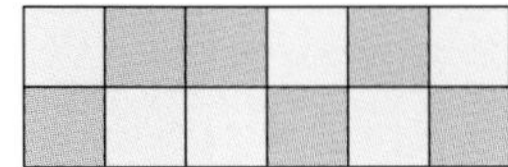

Cream Border Unit Diagram

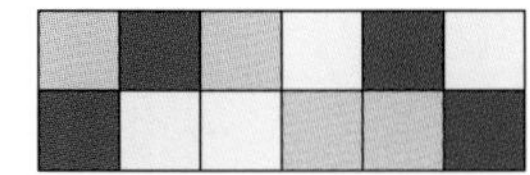

Green Border Unit Diagram

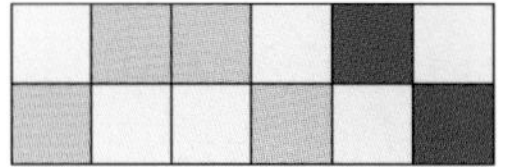

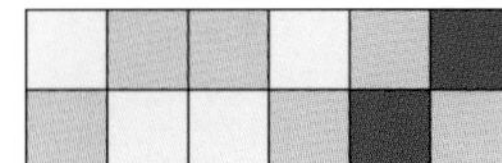

Corner Border Unit Diagrams

Quilt Assembly

1. Lay out Milky Way blocks, Shoo-Fly blocks, and border units as shown in *Quilt Top Assembly Diagram.* Join into rows; join rows to complete quilt center.
2. Add 1 (2" x 96½") cream print border to each side of quilt. Join green C squares to ends of remaining (2" x 78½") borders. Add to top and bottom of quilt.
3. Center 1 (3½" x 108") green border on each side of quilt and join, beginning and ending seams **exactly** ¼" from each corner of quilt top. Backstitch at beginning and ending of stitching to reinforce. Attach 3½" x 90" borders to top and bottom of quilt in the same manner. Fold 1 corner of quilt top diagonally with right sides together and matching edges. Use ruler to mark stitching line as shown in *Mitered Corner Diagram.* Sew on drawn line, backstitching at beginning and ending of stitching. Trim seam allowance to ¼" and press to 1 side. Repeat for other corners.

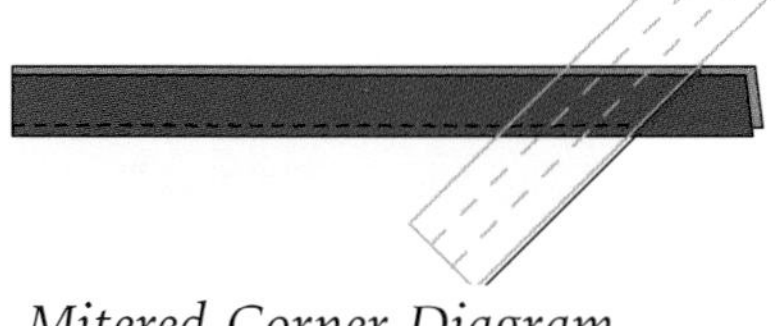

Mitered Corner Diagram

Quilting and Finishing

1. Divide backing fabric into 3 (2¾-yd) lengths. Join along long sides to make backing. Seams will run horizontally.
2. Layer backing, batting, and quilt top; baste. Quilt as desired. Quilt shown was custom machine-quilted.
3. Join 2¼"-wide dark green print strips into 1 continuous piece for straight-grain binding. Follow *Attaching French-Fold Binding with Mitered Corners,* page 79, to add binding to quilt.

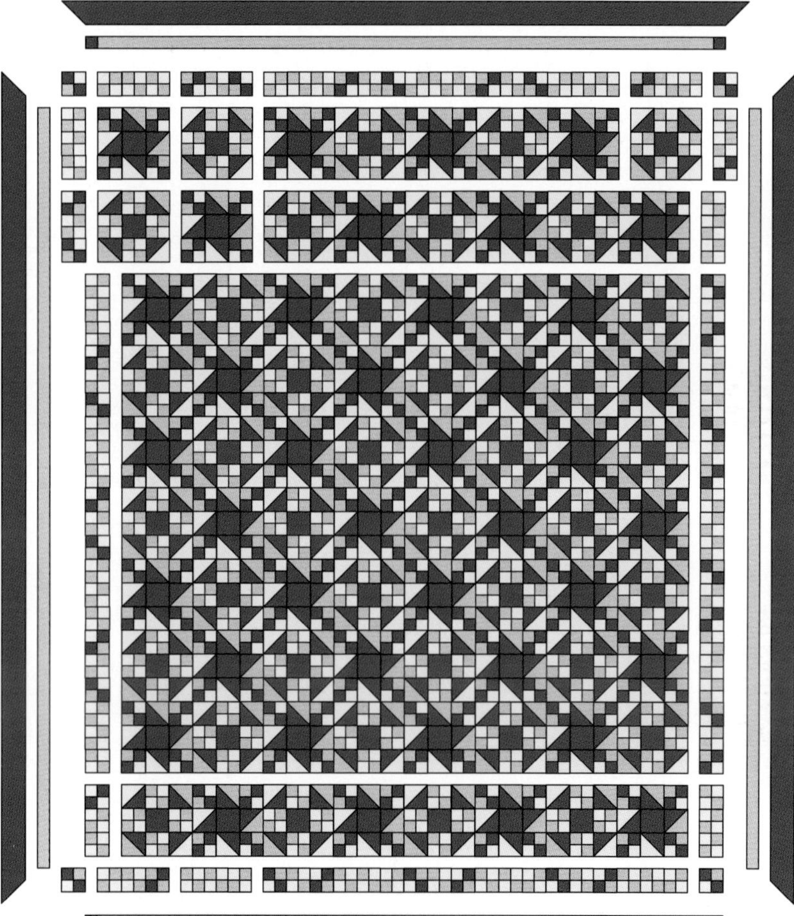

Quilt Top Assembly Diagram

April

The cheerful appeal of springtime *blossoms can be yours any time of the year with this simply beautiful quilt. The swarms of bees in the setting-triangles appear to be gathering nectar from the flower basket blocks, giving the quilt its name.*

The Gathering

Quilt by Susan Ramey Cleveland; quilted by Terry Owens of Classic Quilts (www.classic-quilts.com)

Finished Size: 84" x 98"
Blocks: 50 (10") Basket Blocks

Materials

25 ($6\frac{7}{8}$") squares large-scale blue-and-yellow prints
20 fat quarters* blue prints
20 fat quarters* gold and yellow prints
$1\frac{1}{2}$ yds light medium-scale print for setting triangles
$1\frac{1}{4}$ yds dark gold for inner border and binding
$1\frac{1}{2}$ yds blue print for outer border
$7\frac{1}{2}$ yds fabric for backing
Queen-size batting
Rotary cutter, cutting mat, and acrylic ruler
*Fat quarter = 18" x 22"

Cutting

Measurements include $\frac{1}{4}$" seam allowances. Follow *Rotary Cutting,* page 71. Border strips are exact length needed. You may want to cut them longer to allow for piecing differences.

From 25 print squares:
- Cut squares in half diagonally to make 50 D triangles for blocks.

From each blue fat quarter, cut:
- 1 basket set (total 20 sets):
  - 1 ($6\frac{7}{8}$") square. Cut square in half to make 2 D triangles.
  - 2 ($2\frac{7}{8}$") squares. Cut squares in half to make 4 A triangles.
  - 4 ($2\frac{1}{2}$") B squares.
- 1 or 2 background sets. You will need 30 sets. Cut 1 set from each fat quarter and then another set from 10 more of what remains:
  - 1 ($2\frac{1}{2}$"-wide) strip. Cut strip into 2 ($2\frac{1}{2}$" x $4\frac{1}{2}$") C rectangles and 2 ($2\frac{1}{2}$" x $6\frac{1}{2}$") E rectangles.
  - 1 ($2\frac{7}{8}$") square. Cut square in half diagonally to make 2 A triangles.
  - 1 ($2\frac{1}{2}$") B square.
  - 1 ($4\frac{7}{8}$") square. Cut square in half diagonally to make 2 F triangles. You will have 1 extra.

From gold and yellow fat quarters, cut:
- 1 or 2 basket sets. You will need 30 sets. Cut 1 set from each fat quarter and then another set from 10 more of what remains:
  - 1 ($6\frac{7}{8}$") square. Cut square in half to make 2 D triangles.
  - 2 ($2\frac{7}{8}$") squares. Cut squares in half to make 4 A triangles.
  - 4 ($2\frac{1}{2}$") B squares.
- 1 background set (total 20 sets):
  - 1 ($2\frac{1}{2}$"-wide) strip. Cut strip into 2 ($2\frac{1}{2}$" x $4\frac{1}{2}$") C rectangles and 2 ($2\frac{1}{2}$" x $6\frac{1}{2}$") E rectangles.
  - 1 ($2\frac{7}{8}$") square. Cut square in half diagonally to make 2 A triangles.
  - 1 ($2\frac{1}{2}$") B square.
  - 1 ($4\frac{7}{8}$") square. Cut square in half diagonally to make 2 F triangles. You will have 1 extra.

From light medium-scale print, cut:
- 3 ($15\frac{1}{2}$"-wide) strips. Cut strips into 5 ($15\frac{1}{2}$") squares. Cut squares in quarters diagonally to make 20 side setting triangles. You will have 2 extra.
- From remainder, cut 2 (8") squares. Cut squares in half diagonally to make 4 corner setting triangles.

From dark gold, cut:
- 9 (2"-wide) strips for inner border. Piece strips to make 2 (2" x $85\frac{1}{2}$") side borders and 2 (2" x $74\frac{1}{2}$") top and bottom borders.
- 10 ($2\frac{1}{4}$"-wide) strips for binding.

From blue print, cut:
- 9 ($5\frac{1}{2}$"-wide) strips for outer border. Piece strips to make 2 ($5\frac{1}{2}$" x $88\frac{1}{2}$") side borders and 2 ($5\frac{1}{2}$" x $84\frac{1}{2}$") top and bottom borders.

Block Assembly

1. Choose 1 set each of basket and background pieces (1 yellow, 1 blue), plus 1 large print D triangle.
2. Join 1 basket and 1 background A triangles to make 1 A unit *(A Unit Diagram)*. Make 2 A units.
3. Referring to *Diagonal Seams Diagrams,* place 1 basket B square atop 1 end of 1 background C rectangle. Stitch diagonally, trim excess fabric beyond stitching, and press open. Repeat on opposite end to make 1 Goose Chase unit. Make 2 Goose Chase units.
4. Referring to *Block Assembly Diagram,* join 1 large print D triangle and 1 basket D triangle to make center. Join 1 Goose Chase unit and 1 A unit and add to center unit. Join remaining A unit and Goose Chase unit; add 1 background B square. Add to center.

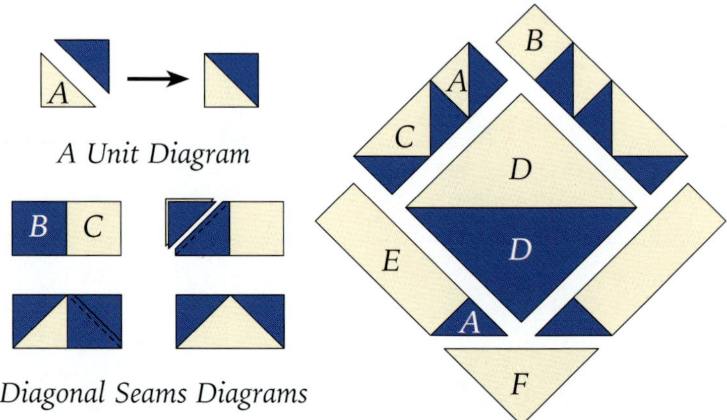

A Unit Diagram

Diagonal Seams Diagrams

Block Assembly Diagram

Tip from Marianne

When you join the A/E unit to the basket, align the square end of the E rectangle with the basket edge. The A triangle will extend slightly beyond the other end, but when you add the other A/E unit, the triangles will intersect perfectly with a 1/4" seam allowance.

5. Join 1 basket A triangle to 1 E rectangle. Add to center as shown. Repeat on adjacent side. Add 1 background F triangle to complete 1 Basket block.
6. Make 50 basket blocks (20 blue baskets with yellow backgrounds, 30 yellow baskets with blue backgrounds).

Quilt Assembly

1. Lay out blocks and setting triangles as shown in *Quilt Top Assembly Diagram*. Join into diagonal rows; join rows to complete quilt center. Trim evenly to 71 1/2" x 85 1/2".
2. Add dark gold side borders to quilt. Add top and bottom borders.
3. Add blue side borders to quilt. Add top and bottom borders.

Quilting and Finishing

1. Divide backing fabric into 3 (2 1/2-yd) lengths. Cut 1 piece in half lengthwise. Sew 1 narrow panel between wide panels. Press seam allowances toward narrow panel. Remaining panel is extra and may be used as a hanging sleeve. Seams will run horizontally.
2. Layer backing, batting, and quilt top; baste. Quilt as desired. Quilt shown was quilted in heart motifs in baskets, outline-quilted in points, and meander quilted in backgrounds. Outer blue border features a vine and leaf pattern.
3. Join 2 1/4"-wide dark gold strips into 1 continuous piece for straight-grain binding. Follow *Attaching French-Fold Binding with Mitered Corners,* page 79, to add binding to quilt.

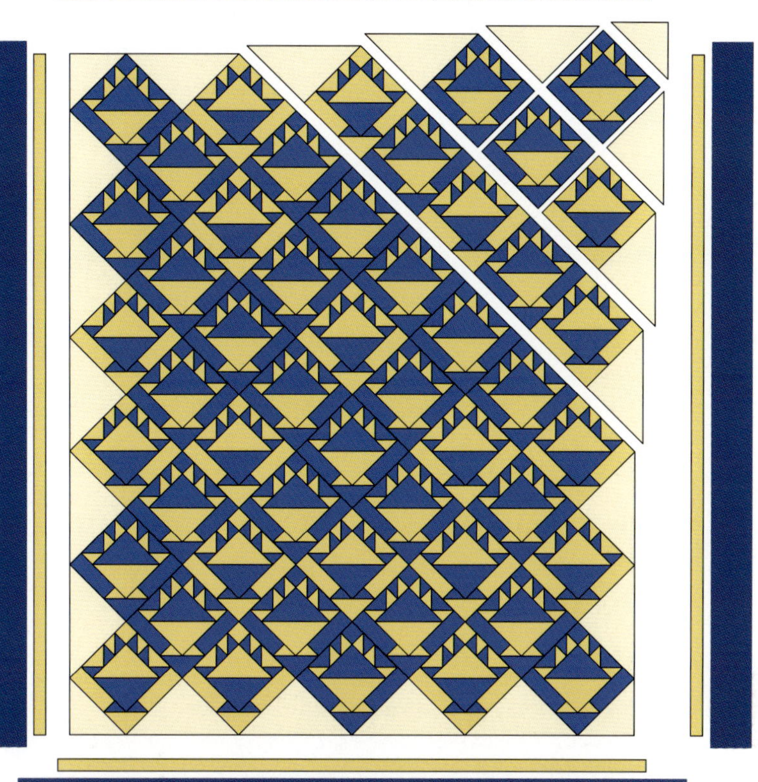

Quilt Top Assembly Diagram

"Bee" Creative

Add a delicate touch to your quilt label by using machine embroidery or a piece of an old handkerchief. Here, Susan Cleveland wrote the year inside an embroidered heart with her name, city, and state in the corners.

May

April showers have brought

May flowers to this quilted garden! The delicate blooms are pieced using Nine-Patch units. A scalloped border adds a hint of feminine style. This delightful quilt was hand-pieced and hand-quilted, but you can stitch the design on your sewing machine.

Flower Garden

Quilt designed and made by Linn Styczenski

Finished Size: Approximately 81" x 108"
Blocks: 54 Flower Units

Materials

9 yds white fabric for background, setting units, and borders
3 yds of green print fabric for borders and binding
54 (2" x 9") strips of assorted pastel print fabrics (pink, yellow, purple, peach, blue) for flowers
54 (2" x 13") strips of assorted green print fabrics for flower leaves
1/4 yd of solid yellow for flower centers
6 1/2 yds of backing fabric
3 1/4 yds of 90"-wide batting
Rotary cutter, acrylic ruler, and cutting mat
Plastic-coated freezer paper at least 81" long
15"-long piece of string and chalk pencil to make compass

Cutting

Measurements for cutting include 1/4" seam allowances. Cut strips selvage-to-selvage unless directed otherwise. Follow *Rotary Cutting,* page 71. Borders are cut longer to allow for mitering corners.

From white fabric, cut:

- 2 (10 1/2" x 112") lengthwise side outer borders.
  2 (10 1/2" x 85") lengthwise top/bottom outer borders.
- 2 (3 1/4" x 89") lengthwise side inner borders.
  2 (3 1/4" x 62") lengthwise top/bottom inner borders.
- 3 (5" x 88") lengthwise strips. From these cut 40 (5") squares for setting blocks.
- 41 (2"-wide) strips. From these, cut 201 (2") squares, 186 (2" x 5") rectangles for setting units, and 34 (2" x 8") rectangles for pieced borders.

From green print, cut:

- 8 (2"-wide) strips for middle border.
- 8 (5" x 56 1/4") lengthwise strips for appliqué border. Reserve remaining fabric for binding.

From each pastel fabric, cut:

- 4 matching 2" squares for flowers (total of 54 sets of 4).

From assorted green prints, cut:

- 6 matching 2" squares for leaves (total of 54 sets of 6).

From yellow fabric, cut;

- 3 (2"-wide) strips. From these, cut 54 (2") squares for flower centers.

Assembly

Making Patchwork Units

1. Referring to *Nine-Patch Assembly Diagrams,* sew matching pastel flower squares to opposite sides of a yellow square for top row, white squares to opposite sides of a flower square for middle row, and 3 matching green squares for bottom row. Join rows. Pin the extra matching flower and green squares to unit. Repeat to make 54 units. Lay out units in 9 horizontal rows of 6 units per row.

Nine-Patch Assembly Diagrams

2. Working with extra pieces from the top left Nine-Patch unit and the Nine-Patch unit to the right of it, join 1 extra green square from each Nine-Patch unit to opposite sides of a 2" white square as shown in *Type A Setting Unit Diagrams.* Stitch a 2" x 5" white rectangle to top and bottom to complete unit. Stitch Nine-Patch units to opposite sides of Type A Setting Unit. Using green squares from adjacent Nine-Patch units, continue to make Type A Setting Units and join blocks along top of quilt into a horizontal row as shown in Type A Row (*Quilt Top Assembly Diagram,* page 27). Repeat to make a total of 9 Type A rows.

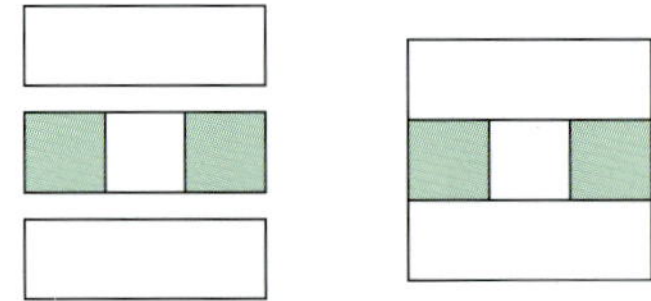

Type A Setting Unit Diagrams

3. Working with extra pieces the top left Nine-Patch unit and the Nine-Patch unit below it, stitch 1 green square from the top Nine-Patch unit and 1 flower square from the Nine-Patch unit below to opposite sides of a 2" white square as shown in *Type B Setting Unit Diagrams.* Stitch a 2" x 5" white rectangle to opposite sides to complete unit. Lay unit between Nine-Patch units. In a similar manner, make Type B Setting Units to place between Nine-Patch units in top 2 Type A rows. Referring to Type B Row, alternately join these Type B Setting Units with 5" white squares. Repeat to make Type B rows to fit between all Type A rows.

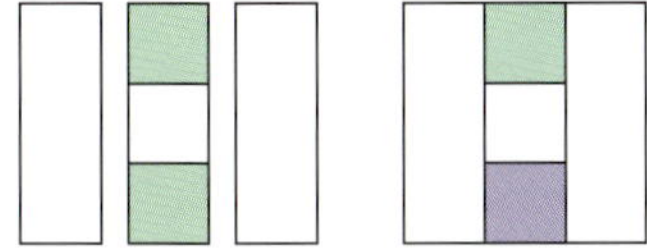

Type B Setting Unit Diagrams

4. Join Type A and Type B rows.
5. To make pieced top border which completes top row of flowers, alternately join extra flower squares and 2" x 8" white rectangles as shown in *Quilt Top Assembly Diagram*. In a similar manner, make pieced borders for bottom and sides of quilt. Stitch borders to quilt, beginning and ending seams **exactly** 1/4" from each corner of quilt top. Backstitch at beginning and ending of stitching to reinforce. Fold one corner of quilt top diagonally with right sides together and matching edges. Use ruler to mark stitching line as shown in *Mitered Corner Diagram*. Sew on drawn line, backstitching at beginning and ending of stitching. Trim seam allowance to 1/4" and press to one side. Repeat for other corners.

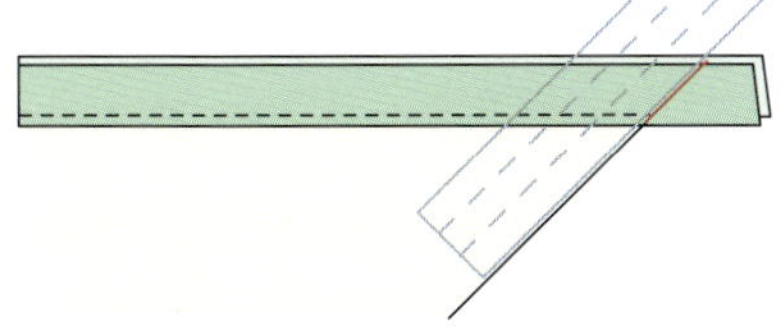

Mitered Corner Diagram

Adding Borders

1. Join 2"-wide green print border strips end to end to form 1 long border strip. Cut 2 (2" x 65") top/bottom border strips and 2 (2" x 92") side border strips. Fold each strip in half crosswise and press to form center mark.

Fan-quilting adds a fanciful touch to this quilt's scalloped border.

2. Fold and press all white border strips in half crosswise and press to form center mark.
3. Matching center crease marks, sew a 3 1/4"-wide border strip to 1 side of a 2" x 65" green border. Center and sew a 10 1/2"-wide white border strip to the opposite side to complete top border strip set. Press seams toward green border. Repeat to make border strip sets for bottom and sides.
4. Placing 3 1/4"-wide white borders toward quilt, stitch border strip sets to quilt and miter border corner seams.
5. Join pairs of 5" x 56 1/4" green borders to make 4 long borders. Trim 2 to 5" x 85". Fold each border in half crosswise and press to form center mark.

6. To make scallop border guides, cut 2 ($3^3/_4$" x 81") strips and 2 ($3^3/_4$" x 54") strips from freezer paper. Along 1 long edge of each 81"-long strip, mark 11 scallops, each approximately $7^3/_8$" long and 1" deep. In a similar manner, mark 7 scallops, each approximately $7^3/_4$" long and 1" each deep, along 1 side of each 54"-long strip. Using paper scissors, cut out scallops on paper strips. Fold each paper strip in half crosswise and crease center mark.
7. Press shiny side of paper guide to right side of each green border strip, matching center marks and aligning straight long edge of paper guide with 1 long raw edge of border strip. Trim away excess green border along scallops, allowing $^3/_{16}$" seam allowance to turn under for appliqué. Leave ends of borders untrimmed.
8. Aligning outer raw edges, pin green borders with paper guides still attached atop wide outer borders. At corners, fold under 1 border at a 45° angle that matches angle of mitered seam of wide white border underneath. Place folded end of green border atop adjacent green border. Appliqué folded edge to underlying green border, taking care not to catch underlying white border. Trim excess ends of green borders.
9. Turn under green borders along scalloped paper guidelines, clipping as needed, and appliqué scalloped edges of green borders to white borders. Remove paper guides.
10. Tie string around chalk pencil to create makeshift compass. Referring to *Scalloped Border Diagram,* measure a $7^3/_4$" radius from outer corner of middle green border to mark corner circle on inner edge of outer green appliqué border. Adjust as needed so corner meets scallop ends smoothly. Trim away green border $^3/_{16}$" from marked corner. Turn under edge and appliqué curve to white border underneath, clipping as needed. Use compass to mark outer curve on corner so green border will be approximately 3" wide. Repeat for each corner.

Quilting and Finishing

1. Divide backing fabric into 2 ($3^1/_4$-yd) lengths. Cut 1 piece in half lengthwise. Sew narrow panel to each side of wide panel. Press seam allowances toward narrow panels.
2. Mark quilting designs on quilt top. Quilt shown was hand-quilted in-the-ditch around flowers and has filled medallions in setting blocks. Green middle border has rope pattern, and scalloped white border is fan-quilted with echo fan pattern in outer green border.

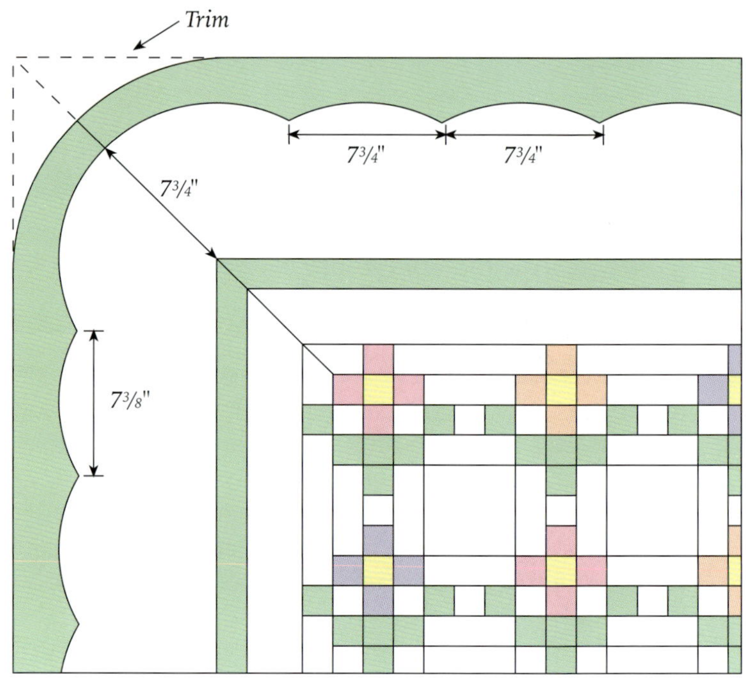

Scalloped Border Diagram

3. Layer backing, batting, and top; baste. Quilt as desired.
4. Make approximately 395" of French-fold bias binding from remaining green print fabric. Stitch binding to quilt following curve guidelines at corners. Trim excess batting and backing. Fold binding to quilt back and slipstitch in place.

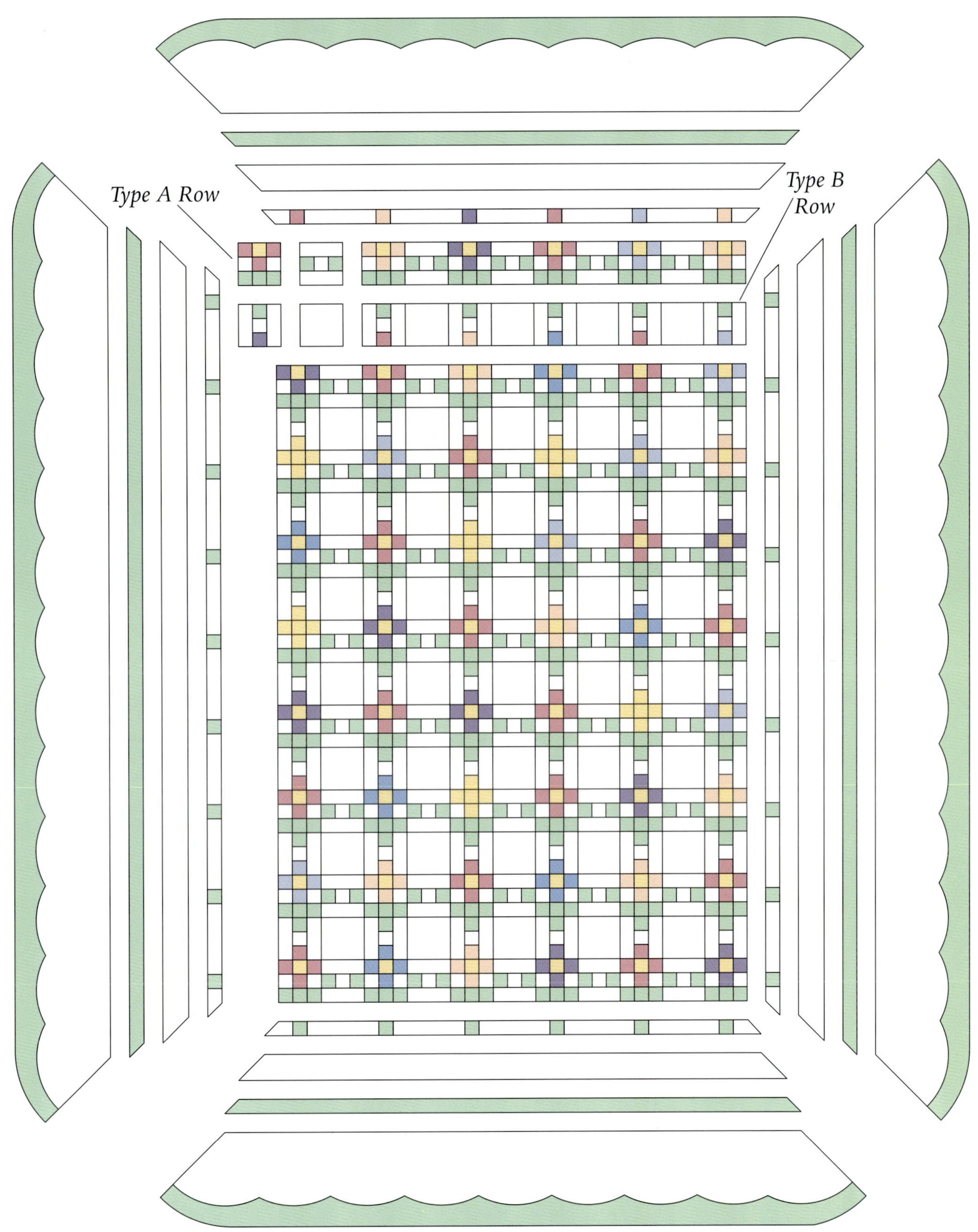

Quilt Top Assembly Diagram

June

Any June bride would be delighted *to receive this peony basket quilt as a wedding gift. Using a cream print for the background of the peony blocks prevents the flowers from getting lost in the pink background. An appliquéd vine winds around the sides and bottom of the quilt.*

Peony Basket

Quilt by Kathy Safris

Finished Size: 86" x 102¼"
Blocks: 20 (12") Blocks

Materials

1½ yds scraps in rose, blue, and purple prints for peonies
¾ yd rose-and-blue print for baskets
1½ yds total assorted greens for leaves and stems
¾ yd green print for bias border vine
2¾ yds white-on-cream print for peony backgrounds
6 yds pink marbled fabric for setting blocks and borders
7¾ yds pink-and-green floral for backing
¾ yd dark pink for binding
90" x 108" queen-size batting
Rotary cutter, mat, and acrylic ruler
Template plastic (You will need to make templates for A, H, and M; patterns are on pages 32-33.)

Cutting

Measurements include ¼" seam allowances. Cut selvage-to-selvage strips unless otherwise noted. Follow *Rotary Cutting*, page 71. Border measurements are exact length needed; you may prefer to cut them longer to allow for piecing variations.

From assorted peony scraps, cut:

- 60 (1¾" x 6½") rectangles. Trim to size, using Template A.
- 30 (2⅝") squares. Cut squares in half diagonally to make 60 triangles (B).
- 30 (3") squares. Cut squares in quarters diagonally to make 120 triangles (C).
- To make pieced border leaves, join scraps randomly by color family into 2" x 4" rectangles *(Leaf Piecing Diagram)*. Cut 31 pieced border leaves, using Template M.

From rose-and-blue print, cut:

- 2 (2⅜"-wide) strips. Cut strips into 20 (2⅜") squares. Cut squares in half diagonally to make 40 triangles (G).
- 2 (6⅜"-wide) strips. Cut strips into 10 (6⅜") squares. Cut squares in half diagonally to make 20 triangles (I).

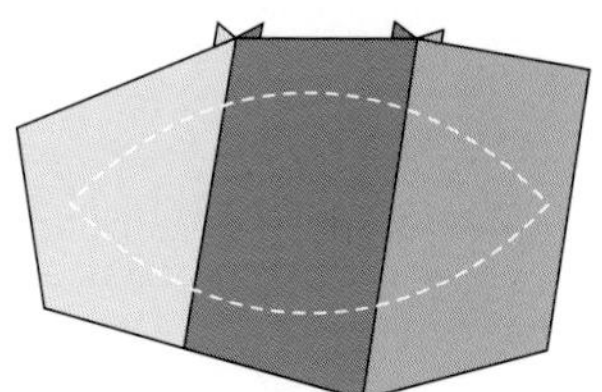

Leaf Piecing Diagram

From assorted greens, cut:

- 136 leaves (M).
- Approximately 14 yards of ¾"-wide bias. Fold in thirds and press to make ¼"-wide finished bias stem for peonies. Cut bias into 60 (8½"-long) pieces for stems L.

From green print, cut:

- Approximately 12 yds of ¾"-wide bias. Fold in thirds and press to make ¼"-wide finished bias vine for border.

From white-on-cream print, cut:

- 3 (3"-wide) strips. Cut strips into 30 (3") squares. Cut squares in quarters diagonally to make 120 triangles (C).
- 4 (2¼"-wide) strips. Cut strips into 60 (2¼") squares (D).
- 4 (4"-wide) strips. Cut strips into 40 (4") squares (E).
- 4 (2"-wide) strips. Cut strips into 40 (2" x 4") rectangles (F).
- 7 (2"-wide) strips. Cut strips into 40 (2" x 6¾") rectangles; trim to size using Template H to make 20 Hs and 20 Reverse Hs.
- 1 (3⅞"-wide) strip. Cut strip into 10 (3⅞") squares. Cut squares in half diagonally to make 20 triangles (J).
- 3 (9⅜"-wide) strips. Cut strips into 10 (9⅜") squares. Cut squares in half diagonally to make 20 triangles (K).

From pink, cut:

- 1 (91"-long) lengthwise strip. From this cut:
    - 1 (5¾" x 68½") rectangle for tuck strip.
    - 2 (9½" x 90¾") rectangles for side borders.
    - 1 (9½" x 86½") rectangle for bottom border.
    - 1 (3½" x 86½") rectangle for top border.
- 3 (12½"-wide) strips. Cut strips into 9 (12½") squares for setting blocks (X).
- 1 (9⅜"-wide) strip. Cut strip into 4 (9⅜") squares. Cut squares in half diagonally to make 8 corner triangles (Z).
- 3 (18¼"-wide) strips. Cut strips into 5 (18¼") squares. Cut squares in quarters diagonally to make 18 edge setting triangles (Y). (You will have 2 extra.)

The blocks along the sides of this quilt are turned out to allow the baskets of peonies to cascade off the sides of the bed.

Making Blocks

1. For each peony block, choose a color family and lay out 3 As, 3 Bs, and 6 Cs. You will also need 6 Cs, 3 Ds, 2 Es, 2 Fs, 1 K, 1 H, 1 Reverse H, and 1 J in white; 1 I and 2 Gs in rose-and-blue print; 3 bias stems L, cutting lengths as needed; and 4 leaves M in assorted greens.
2. Referring to *Peony Assembly Diagram*, join short side of 1 A to long side of 1 B. Repeat to make 3 triangular units.

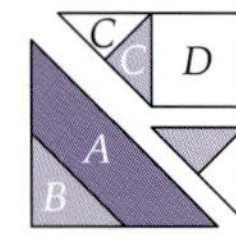

Peony Assembly Diagram

3. Refer to *Peony Assembly Diagram* to join a colored C to a white C to make triangle. Make 3 units with white on right and 3 units with white on left as shown.
4. Join 1 C triangle unit to 2 sides of 1 D square as shown. Join to A/B unit to complete peony unit as shown. Repeat to make 3 units.
5. Following *Block Placement Diagram,* join 1 G to square end of 1 H to make a parallelogram. Repeat with remaining G and Reverse H. Join to sides of I. Join J to Gs to complete basket unit triangle.
6. Stitch basket unit to K.
7. Join 1 E, 1 peony unit, and 1 F; sew to side of block. Join 1 F, 1 peony unit, 1 E, and 1 peony unit; sew to top of block.
8. Following photo, position and appliqué 3 stems L to block so that ends meet peonies and basket. Position and appliqué 4 leaves M. Vary stem and leaf placement for each block.
9. Repeat to make 20 blocks.

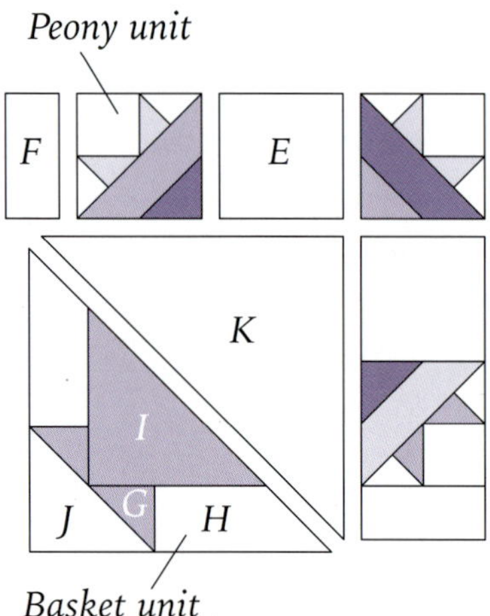

Block Assembly Diagram

Assembly

1. Referring to *Quilt Top Assembly Diagram,* page 33, lay out blocks and setting pieces as shown, taking care to turn peony blocks as shown.
2. Join Y and Z triangles and 4 blocks to make pillow tuck. Sew pillow tuck strip to lower edge.
3. Join 16 blocks and X, Y, and Z setting pieces into diagonal rows for main portion of quilt. Join rows. Stitch this portion of quilt to lower edge of pillow tuck strip.
4. Join side borders to quilt top. Add bottom border to quilt. Add top border to quilt.
5. Referring to photo, position and appliqué vine, green leaves, and pieced border leaves to borders.

Quilting and Finishing

1. Mark desired quilting design.
2. Divide backing fabric into 3 (92"-long) lengths. Join pieces. Seams will run parallel to top and bottom edges of quilt.
3. Layer backing, batting, and quilt top. Baste. Quilt as desired.
4. From binding fabric, make approximately 480" of straight-grain binding. Refer to *Attaching French-Fold Binding with Mitered Corners,* page 79, to add binding to quilt.

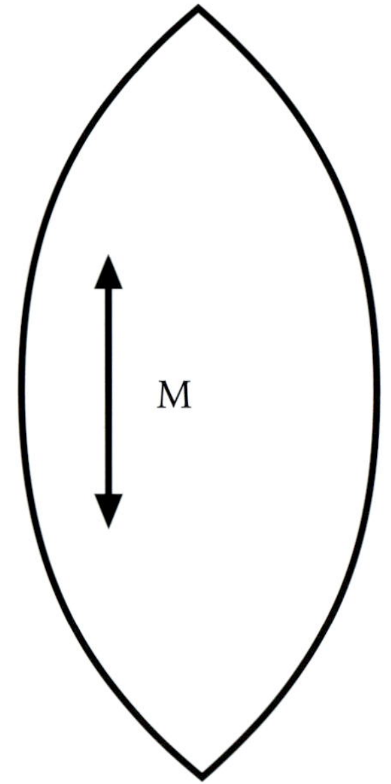

Note: Pattern M is finished size; be sure to add seam allowance when cutting fabric.

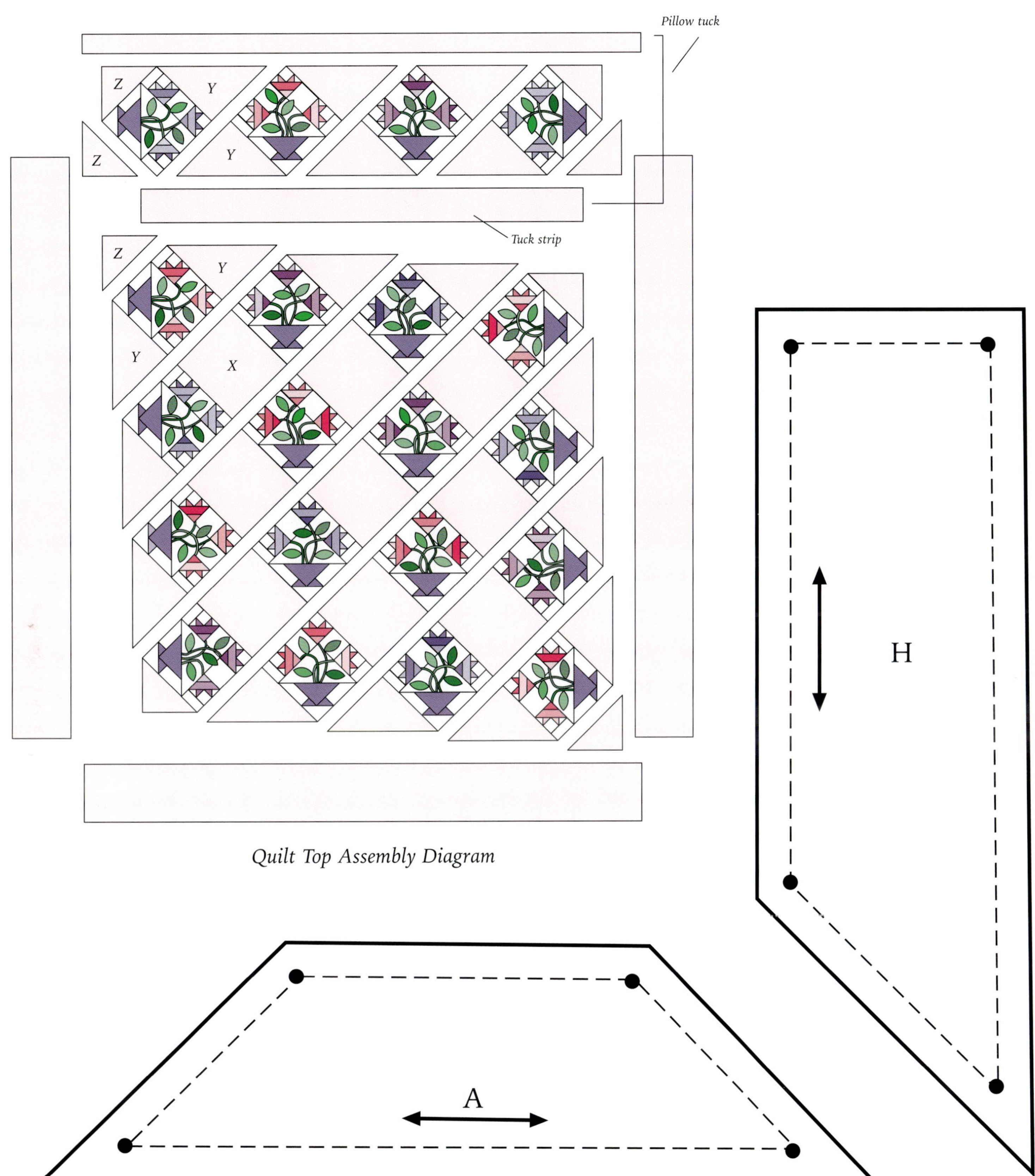

Quilt Top Assembly Diagram

July

Celebrate our nation's independence

with a quilt highlighted by stars and stripes. Drape it over a chair for a fitting Fourth of July tribute, or take it along on a sunny picnic or to a fireworks display. Use country colors like the version shown here, or try bright novelty prints for spirited flair.

Stars & Stripes

Quilt by Andria Grant

Finished Size: 68¼" x 92⅝"
Blocks: 3 (16¼" x 24⅜") Flag Blocks and 36 (8⅛") Triangle Blocks

Materials

18 (9") blue print squares for blocks
18 (9") light print squares for blocks
¼ yd blue print for star field
¾ yd red print for flag stripes
½ yd light print for flag stripes
¼ yd gold print for stars
2⅜ yds blue print for borders
½ yd light print for border
¾ yd red for binding
5½ yds fabric for backing
Twin-size batting
Fusible webbing
Rotary cutter, cutting mat, and acrylic ruler

Cutting

Measurements include ¼" seam allowances. Border strips are exact length needed. You may want to cut them longer to allow for piecing variations. Star pattern is on pages 38 and 39. Follow *Rotary Cutting,* page 71.

From blue print for star field, cut:
- 3 (8" x 10½") rectangles.

From red print for flag stripes, cut:
- 12 (1¾"-wide) strips. Cut strips into 12 (1¾" x 24⅞") strips and 9 (1¾" x 14⅞") strips.

From light print for flag stripes, cut:
- 9 (1¾"-wide) strips. Cut strips into 9 (1¾" x 24⅞") strips and 9 (1¾" x 14⅞") strips.

From gold print:
- Fuse webbing to back of fabric following manufacturer's instructions. Cut 3 stars.

From blue print for borders, cut:
- 4 (2½"-wide) lengthwise strips. Cut strips into 2 (2½" x 73⅝") side inner borders and 2 (2½" x 53¼") top and bottom borders.
- 4 (6½"-wide) lengthwise strips. Cut strips into 2 (6½" x 81⅛") side outer borders and 2 (6½" x 68¾") top and bottom outer borders.

From light for border, cut:
- 7 (2¼"-wide) strips. Piece to make 2 (2¼" x 77⅝") side borders and 2 (2¼" x 56¾") top and bottom borders.

From red for binding, cut:
- 9 (2¼"-wide) strips for binding.

Block Assembly

1. Draw a diagonal line across wrong side of 1 light square. Place 1 light square atop 1 blue square, with right sides facing. Stitch ¼" from drawn line on both sides as shown in *Diagram 1.* Cut on drawn line and press seam allowances to blue fabric. This makes 2 half-square triangle blocks *(Diagram 2).* Make 36 half-square triangle blocks.

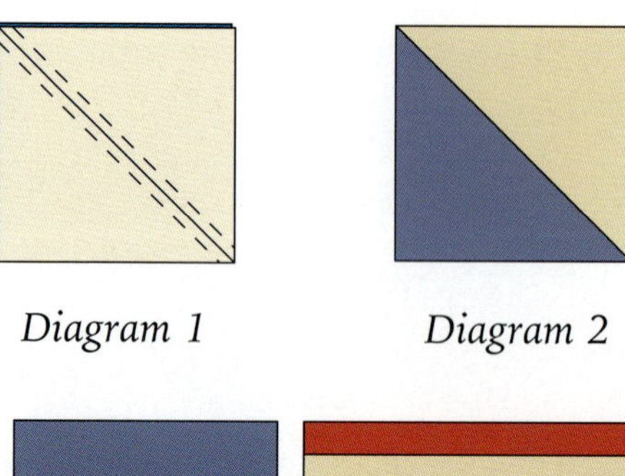

Diagram 1 *Diagram 2*

Block Assembly Diagram

Block Diagram

2. Referring to *Block Assembly Diagram,* join 3 red and 3 light (1¾" x 14⅞") strips as shown to make upper flag section. Add 1 (8" x 10½") rectangle to left side to make upper section of flag. Join 4 red and 3 light (1¾" x 24⅞") strips to make lower section of flag. Join sections to make 1 flag block *(Block Diagram).* Repeat to make 3 flag blocks. Flags should measure 16¾" x 24⅞" with seam allowances.
3. Fuse stars in place. Appliqué edges with buttonhole stitch, page 50.

Quilt Assembly

1. Lay out blocks and flags as shown in *Quilt Top Assembly Diagram,* rotating blue corners of blocks to form stripes. Working in sections, join blocks into rows; join rows. Join sections as shown to complete quilt center.
2. Add blue inner side borders. Add blue top and bottom borders.
3. Add light side borders. Add light top and bottom borders.
4. Add blue outer side borders. Add blue top and bottom borders.

Quilting and Finishing

1. Divide backing fabric into 2 (2³/₄-yd) lengths. Cut 1 piece in half lengthwise. Sew 1 narrow panel to each side of wide panel. Press seam allowances toward narrow panels.
2. Layer backing, batting, and quilt top; baste. Quilt as desired. Quilt shown has meander quilting all over.
3. Join 2¹/₄"-wide red strips into 1 continuous piece for straight-grain binding. Follow *Attaching French-Fold Binding with Mitered Corners,* page 79, to add binding to quilt.

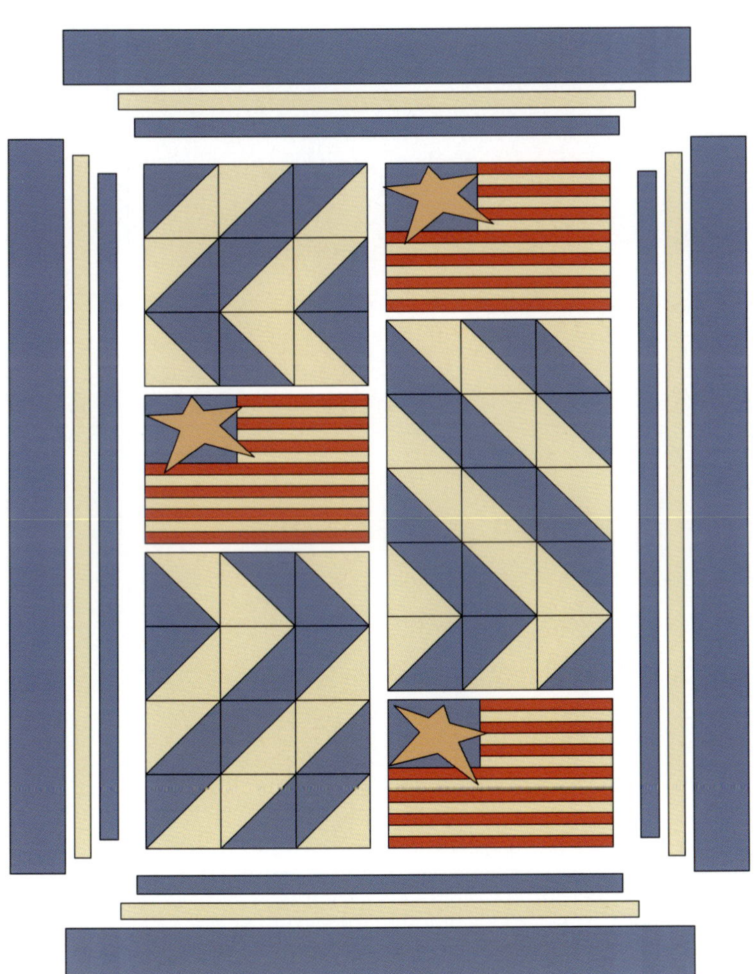

Quilt Top Assembly Diagram

Angled stripes of contrasting blue and white prints make a dramatic backdrop for the stylized flags.

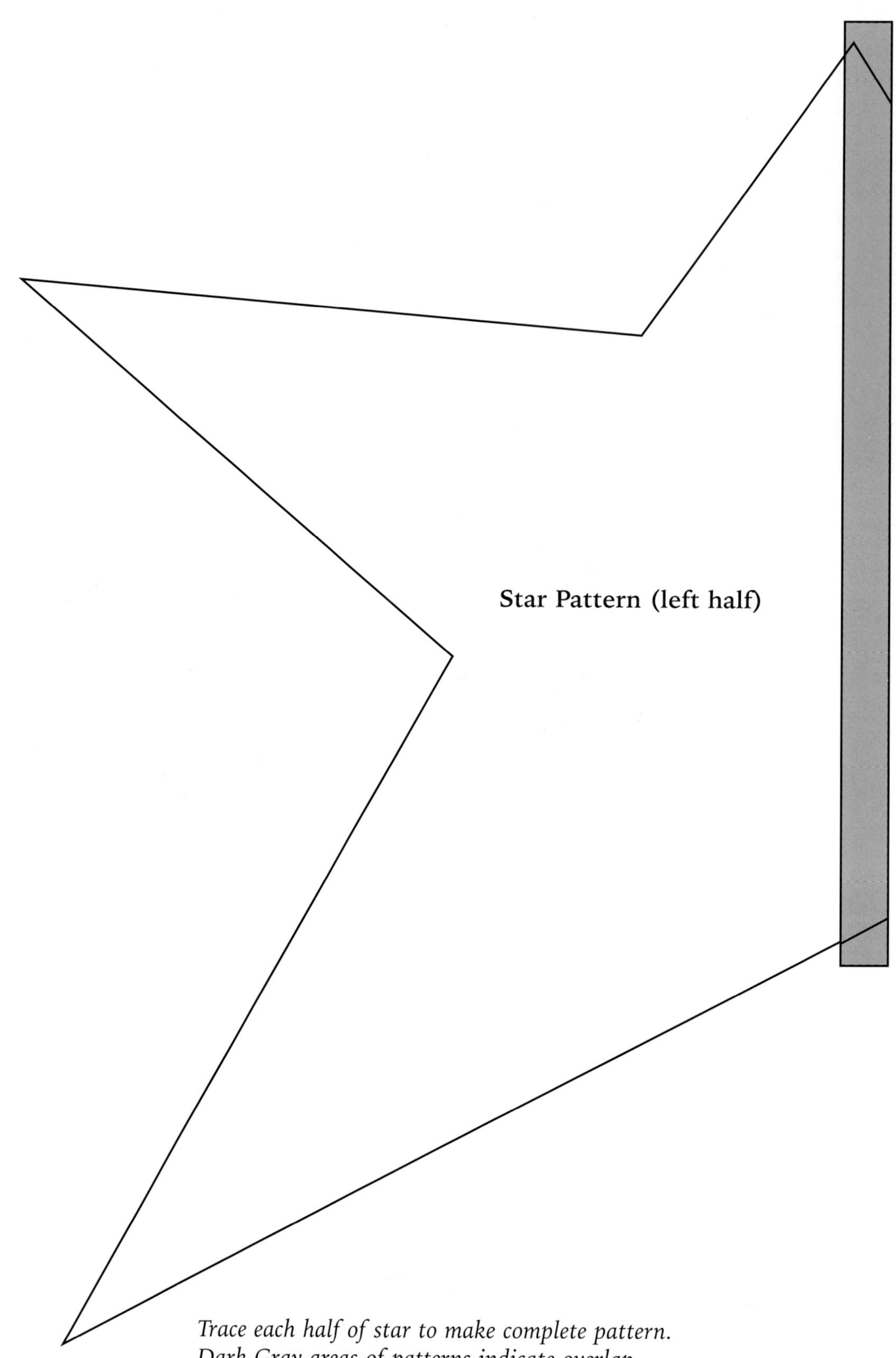

Trace each half of star to make complete pattern.
Dark Gray areas of patterns indicate overlap.

Try This!
Pattern tester Cynthia Moody Wheeler used Fons & Porter's "Belle France" fabric collection by Benartex to make her flag.

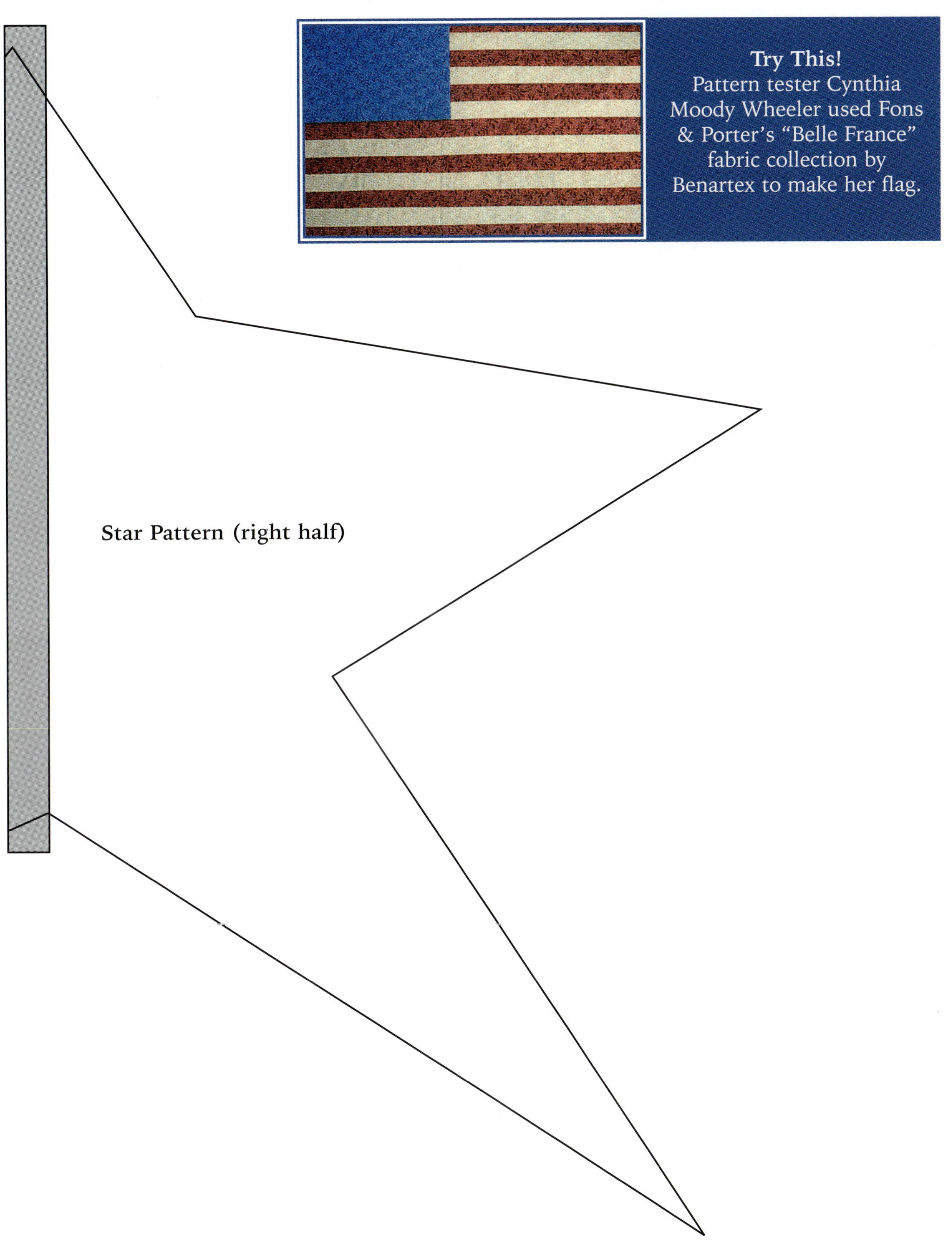

August

Showcasing floral rays of sunshine, *this quilt is sure to brighten your day! The appliquéd blocks feature sunflowers that peek out from behind green leaf stems. The design is pieced in warm, inviting tones and topped off with a bold coordinating border fabric.*

Sunflower Sayonara

Quilt designed by Terri Shinn of Snohomish, Washington, from friends' blocks by the Anchorage (Alaska) Log Cabin Quilters; quilted by Tammy Christman

Finished Size: 77" x 87"
Blocks: 42 (10") blocks

Materials

42 (11") assorted red squares
42 (10" x 18") assorted green scraps
42 (10") assorted yellow squares
42 (3½" x 6") assorted brown/black scraps
¾ yd fabric for middle border
2½ yds fabric for outer border
1 yd fabric for binding
5½ yds fabric for backing
Full/queen batting

Block Assembly

Make templates of patterns B-L on pages 44 and 45. Use a ⅛" hole-punch or a large needle to punch dots in templates as indicated on patterns.

1. Cut 1 red square in half diagonally to make 2 triangles. Set aside 1 triangle for A. From second triangle, cut 1 each of G, I, and K as shown *(Diagram A)*.

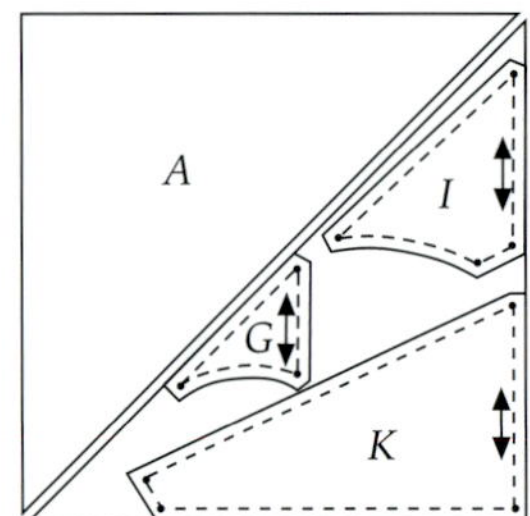

Diagram A

2. Cut a 3½" x 10" strip from 1 yellow fabric square and set aside for border. Adding seam allowance, cut 1 each of B, C, D, and E from remainder of yellow square. Cut 1 F from black scrap. Leaving bottom edges flat, turn under seam allowances on each piece.
3. Pin pieces onto A, referring to photo and diagrams for placement. Align raw edge of F with diagonal edge of A triangle, and position points of B, C, D, and E a scant ½" from perpendicular edges of triangle. When satisfied with placement, appliqué pieces in place in alphabetical order, overlapping subsequent pieces as shown on pattern. Press appliquéd triangle and set aside.
4. Cut a 7" x 10" strip from 1 green scrap and set aside for border. From remaining fabric, cut 1 each of H, J, and L. Mark dots on wrong side of each piece.
5. Matching dots, pin G to H. Join curved edges of G and H *(Block Assembly Diagram)* piecing by hand or machine. If you have trouble piecing this curved seam, you can turn under seam allowance on H and appliqué edge to G. Press seam allowance toward G.

Block Assembly Diagram *Sunflower Block—Make 42.*

6. Stitch I to bottom edge of H as shown. Press seam allowance toward I.
7. Piece or appliqué curved edge of J to bottom of H/I, matching dots. Press seam allowance toward J.
8. Stitch K to bottom edge of I/J. Press seam allowance toward K.
9. Join stem section to appliquéd triangle, aligning sections at top right corner of block (Triangle A is longer than stem section.) Press seam allowance toward A.
10. Align ruler with raw edge of J/K at bottom left corner of block. With ruler in position, use a rotary cutter to trim corner of A triangle.
11. Sew L to A/J/K corner to complete block. Press seam allowance toward L. Trim block to 10½" x 10½".
12. Make 42 Sunflower blocks in this manner.

Quilt Assembly

1. Lay out 7 horizontal rows of 6 blocks each *(Row Assembly Diagram)*. Rearrange blocks as desired to achieve a pleasing balance of color and value. When satisfied with placement, join blocks in each row.
2. Join rows, referring to *Quilt Top Diagram* on page 43.

Row Assembly Diagram

Border Assembly

Before cutting, read instructions and decide whether you prefer diagonal seams quick-piecing technique or traditional piecing for flying geese. Instructions are for rotary cutting. (Refer to *Rotary Cutting*, page 71.) For traditional cutting, use patterns M and N on pages 44 and 45 for templates.

1. From remaining green fabrics, cut 56 (3" x 5½") pieces to make geese with diagonal seams or 56 of Template M for traditional piecing.
2. From remaining yellow fabrics, cut 104 (3") squares to make geese with diagonal seams or 104 of Template N for traditional piecing.
3. Use diagonal seams to join 2 yellow squares to 1 green rectangle *(Diagram B)*. Or sew N triangles to M triangle traditionally as shown. Make 48 flying geese.
4. Add a triangle corner to 1 corner only of remaining 8 M pieces, sewing 4 left corners and 4 right corners as shown *(Diagram C)*.

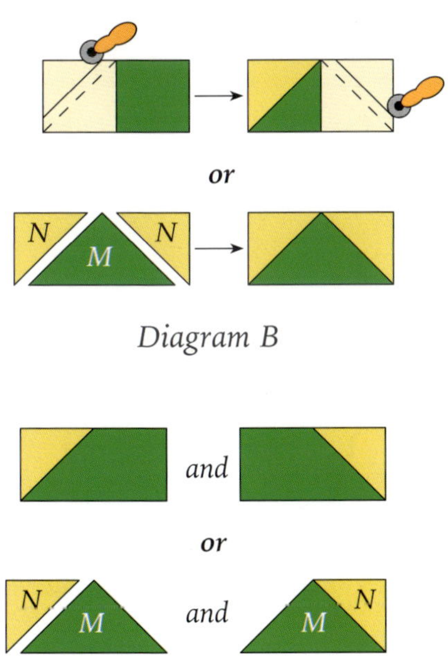

5. Referring to *Quilt Top Diagram*, join 13 flying geese end-to-end in a row for each side border. In same manner, join 11 flying geese in a row for top and bottom borders. Add a corner unit to both ends of each row.
6. Join borders to quilt edges, easing to fit as needed. Miter border corners.
7. For middle border, cut 8 (2½"-wide) crosswise strips. Join 2 strips end-to-end to make each border.
8. Measure quilt from top to bottom and trim 2 middle borders to match length. Join border strips to quilt sides.
9. Measure quilt from side to side and trim remaining middle borders to match quilt width. Join borders to top and bottom edges of quilt.
10. From outer border fabric, cut 4 (4½"-wide) lengthwise borders trips. Measure quilt, trim, and sew outer borders as for middle borders.

Quilting and Finishing

1. Mark quilting design on quilt top as desired. Quilt shown is outline-quilted with details on appliqué pieces as shown on patterns.
2. Cut backing into 2 equal lengths. Cut 1 piece in half lengthwise. Join a narrow panel to each side of wide piece to assemble backing.
3. Layer backing, batting, and quilt top. Baste. Quilt as desired.
4. Make 9⅜ yds of bias or straight-grain binding. Follow *Attaching French-Fold Binding with Mitered Corners*, page 79, to add binding to quilt.

Quilt Top Diagram

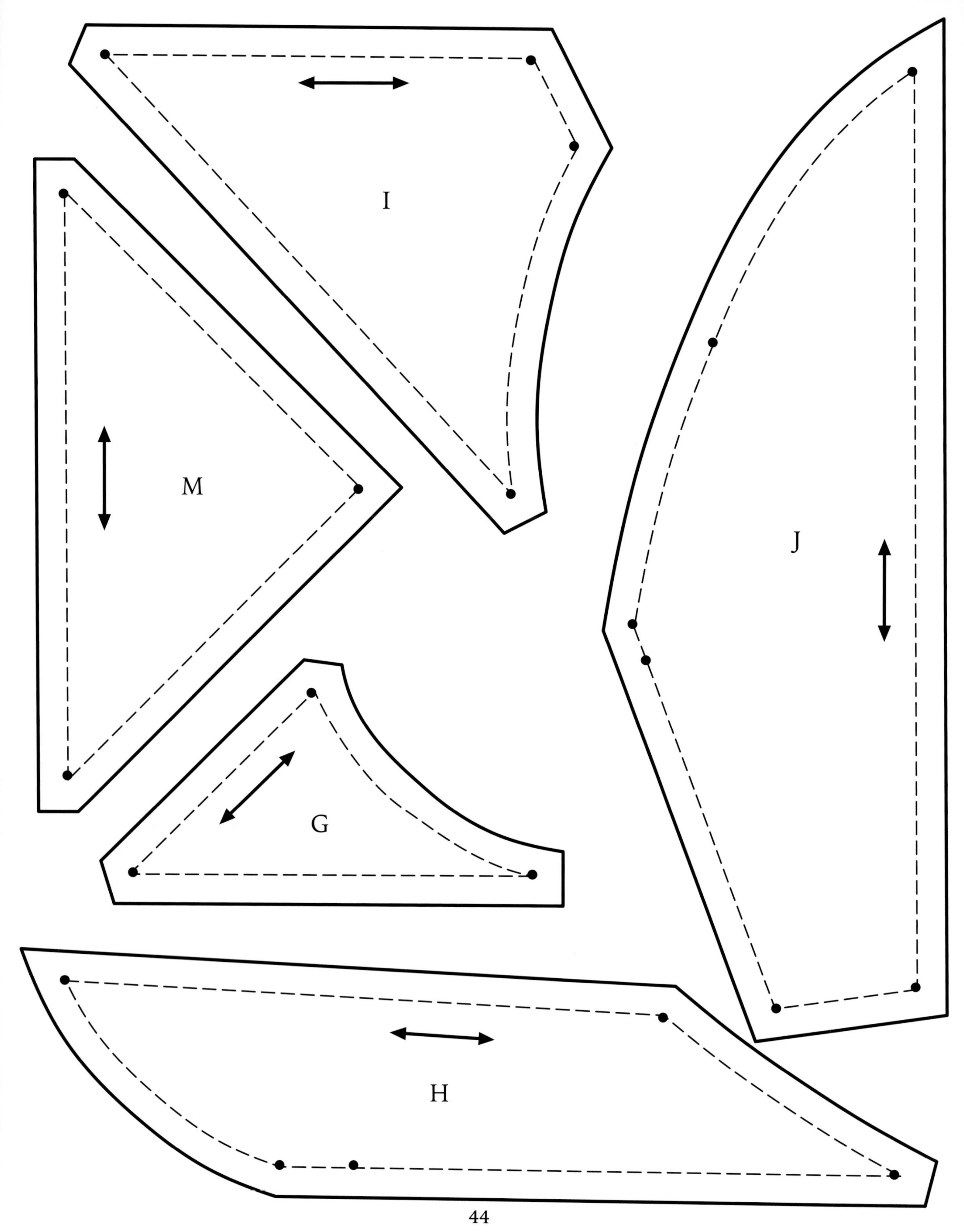
I
M
J
G
H

Note: Patterns B-F are shown finished size; add 1/4" seam allowance when cutting out these appliqué pieces. Broken lines indicate quilting details.

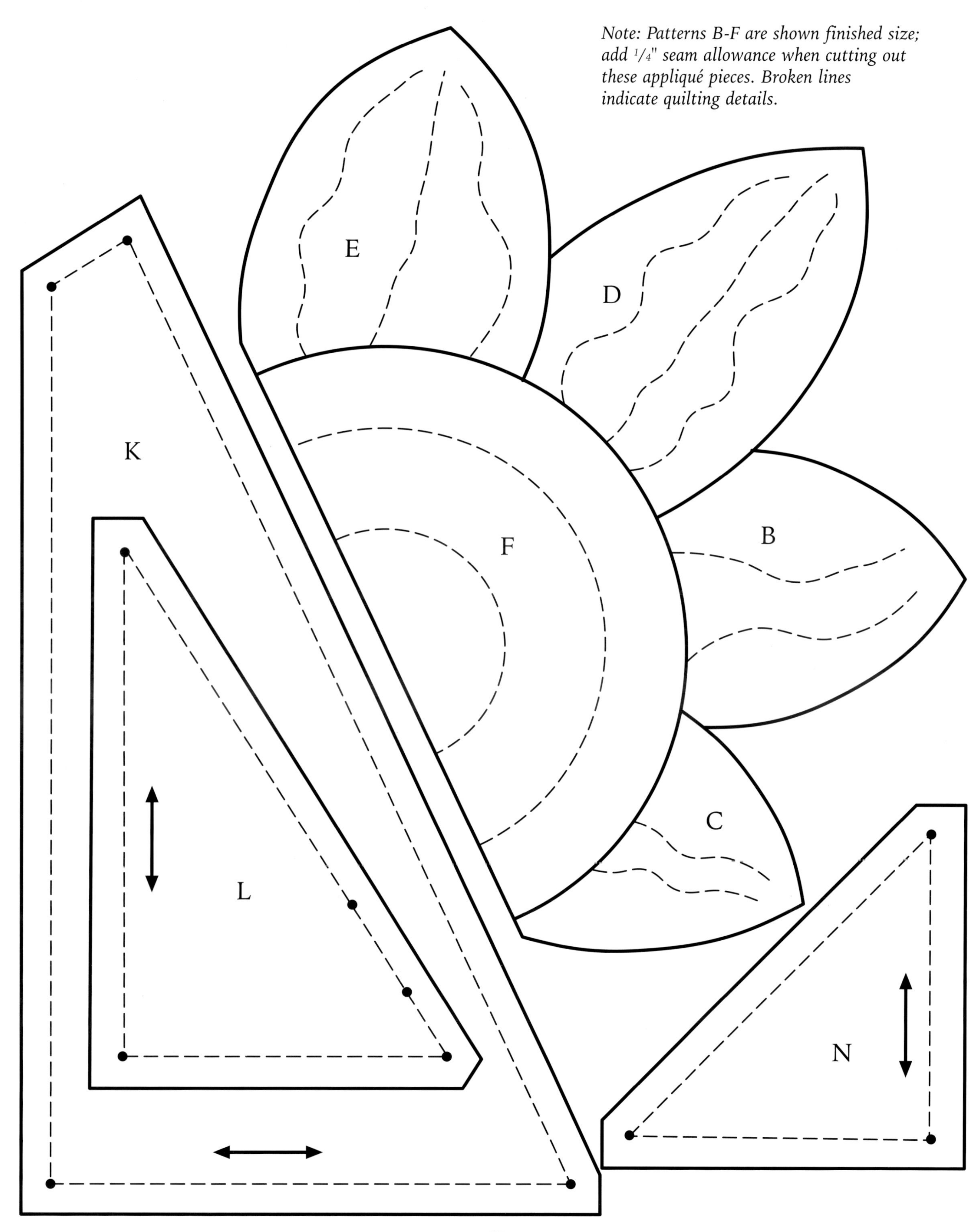

September

Capture the fun of harvest time

as you make this whimsical wall quilt. A bounty of embroidery stitches, sewn by hand or by machine, lends just the right embellishment to the rows of corn and chickens. For a fun finishing touch, the quilt is framed with traditional Hens and Chicks blocks.

Lost in the Cornfield

Quilt by Kris Kerrigan of Button Weeds™

Finished Size: 36" x 48"
Blocks: 52 (3") Hens and Chicks Blocks

Materials

1 yd cream stripe for center
6 fat eighths* assorted cream stripes/plaids for outer border
1 fat quarter** each black, brick red, rust #1, rust #2, and gold stripes or plaids for outer border, ears of corn, and chickens
3 fat eighths* assorted green plaids for cornstalks
1 ($2\frac{1}{2}$" x $10\frac{1}{2}$") strip bright red stripe or plaid for comb/wattle
$\frac{1}{4}$ yd brown stripe for inner border
$\frac{3}{8}$ yd green plaid for binding
$1\frac{1}{2}$ yds fabric for backing
$1\frac{1}{2}$ yds paper-backed fusible web
Taupe #8 pearl cotton threat for big-stitch quilting
Green, rust, gold, and black embroidery floss
10 ($\frac{3}{8}$") dark buttons for chicken eyes
12 ($\frac{3}{8}$") gold buttons for corn kernels
Crib-size batting
Rotary cutter, cutting mat, and acrylic ruler
*Fat eighth = 9" x 22"
** Fat quarter = 18" x 22"

Cutting

Measurements include $\frac{1}{4}$" seam allowances. Cut crosswise strips unless otherwise noted. Follow *Rotary Cutting*, page 71. Inner border strips are exact length needed so outer pieced border will fit. Patterns are on page 51.

From cream stripe, cut:

- 1 ($28\frac{1}{2}$" x $40\frac{1}{2}$") piece for center panel.

From each cream stripe/plaid fat eighth, cut:

- 13 ($2\frac{3}{8}$") squares. Cut squares in half diagonally to make 156 C triangles for outer border.

From each black, brick red, rust, and gold fat quarter, cut:

- 1 ($3\frac{1}{2}$") square for chicken body (E).
- 1 ($1\frac{7}{8}$") square for chicken wing (F).
- 6 ($2\frac{3}{8}$") squares. Cut squares in half diagonally to make 60 C triangles for border. You will have 8 extra.
- 6 ($3\frac{7}{8}$") squares. Cut squares in half diagonally to make 60 D triangles. You will have 8 extra.

Fuse paper-backed fusible web to $4\frac{1}{2}$"-square gold scrap. From this, cut:

- 3 pieces of corn.

Fuse paper-backed fusible web to each green fat eighth. From each, cut:

- 6 cornstalks (A).
- 1 cornstalk with ripe corn (A + B).

Fuse a 2" x 10" piece of paper backed fusible web to bright red stripe or plaid. From this:

- Cut strip into 5 ($1\frac{7}{8}$") squares. Cut squares in half diagonally to make 10 comb/wattle triangles (F).

From brown stripe, cut:

- 4 ($1\frac{1}{2}$"-wide) strips. Cut strips into 2 ($1\frac{1}{2}$" x $40\frac{1}{2}$") side borders and 2 ($1\frac{1}{2}$" x $30\frac{1}{2}$") top and bottom borders.

From $\frac{3}{8}$ yd green plaid, cut:

- 5 ($2\frac{1}{4}$"-wide) strips for binding.

From paper-backed fusible web, cut:

- 5 ($3\frac{1}{4}$") squares. Fuse to wrong side of each $3\frac{1}{2}$" square cut from fat quarters. Cut each square in half diagonally to make 10 chicken bodies (E).
- 5 ($1\frac{5}{8}$") squares. Fuse to wrong side of each $1\frac{7}{8}$" square cut from fat quarters. Cut each square in half diagonally to make 10 chicken wings (F).

Center Appliqué Instructions

1. Remove paper backing from fusible appliqué pieces. At bottom of cream stripe background, beginning $2\frac{3}{4}$" from each side edge and $\frac{1}{4}$" from bottom edge, position 6 cornstalks (A) and 1 cornstalk with ripe corn (A + B). Space cornstalks evenly apart, about $\frac{3}{4}$". When satisfied with placement, fuse in place.
2. Using a pencil, draw a line $1\frac{1}{2}$" above tops of cornstalks. Place 5 chicken bodies (E) $\frac{1}{4}$" above line. Space triangles evenly. Position comb/wattle triangles (F) under each triangle, as shown in *Chicken Block Diagram,* so that chickens are running to the left. Fuse E and F triangles in place. Center each matching chicken wing triangle (F) on chicken body and fuse.

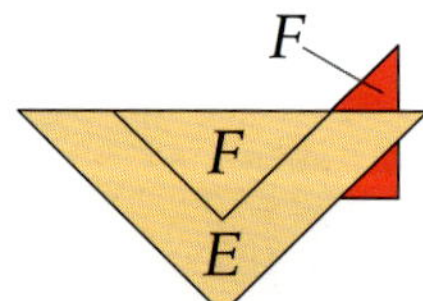

Chicken Block Diagram

3. Draw a line $4\frac{1}{4}$" above previous line. Place bottom of 7 cornstalks on this line, using same spacing as in Step 1 and placing 6 A cornstalks and 1 cornstalk with ripe corn. Fuse.
4. Repeat Step 2 for second row of chickens, placing comb/wattle so that chickens are running to the right. Fuse.
5. Repeat Step 3 for top row of cornstalks, placing 6 A cornstalks and 1 cornstalk with ripe corn. Fuse in place.

Embellishments

Use 2 strands of floss for embroidery. Embroidery diagrams are on page 50.

1. Appliqué all fused pieces to background, using buttonhole stitch and black floss *(Buttonhole-Stitch Diagram)*.
2. Draw 3 (1 1/8"-long) tassel lines at top of each cornstalk. Lines should meet in top center of each cornstalk. Stemstitch with green floss as shown in *Stemstitch Diagram*. Feather-stitch in gold over tassel lines *(Feather-Stitch Diagram)*.
3. Buttonhole-stitch horizontal marked lines under cornstalks for ground. Embroider lines beneath chickens, using running stitch.
4. Referring to *Chicken Diagram* on page 51 and using a pencil, lightly mark tail feathers and legs for each chicken. Backstitch tail feathers with floss to match bodies; backstitch legs and toes with black floss *(Backstitch Diagram)*.
5. Add dark buttons for chicken eyes and gold buttons for corn kernels as shown in photo.

Hens and Chicks Block Assembly

1. Referring to *Block Assembly Diagram*, join 1 dark C and 1 light C to make 1 triangle-square. Join 1 C triangle to dark sides of triangle-square to make large triangle. Join to D triangle to complete 1 Hens and Chicks block *(Block Diagram)*.
2. Make 52 Hens and Chicks blocks, mixing colors as desired.

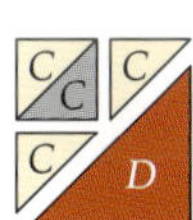

Block Assembly Diagram

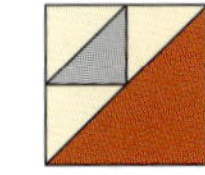

Block Diagram

Quilt Assembly

1. Add 1 (1 1/2" x 40 1/2") brown stripe border to each side of center appliquéd panel. Add 1 (1 1/2" x 30 1/2") brown stripe border to top and bottom of panel.
2. Join 14 Hens and Chicks blocks into a strip as shown in *Quilt Top Assembly Diagram*. Join to 1 side of quilt. Repeat for opposite side.
3. Join 12 Hens and Chicks blocks into a strip as shown in *Quilt Top Assembly Diagram*. Join to top of quilt. Repeat for bottom border.

Quilting and Finishing

1. Layer backing, batting, and quilt top; baste.
2. Quilt as desired. Quilt shown was utility-quilted using big stitch 1/8" from edges of cornstalks and chickens, on each side of inner border, and on outside long edge of D triangles.
3. Join 2 1/4"-wide green plaid strips in 1 continuous piece for straight-grain binding. Follow *Attaching French-Fold Binding with Mitered Corners,* page 79, to add binding to quilt.

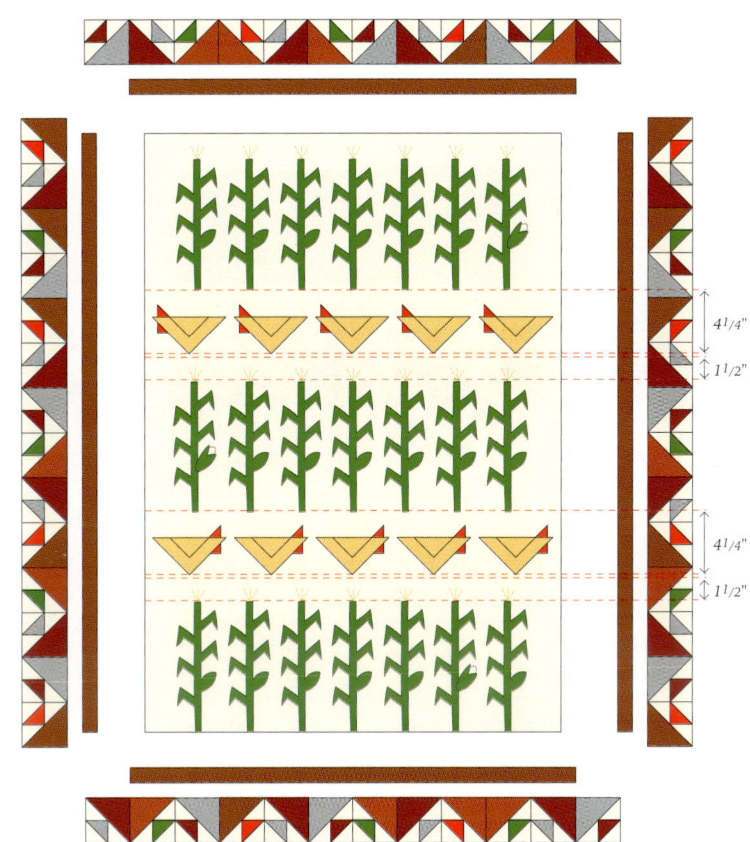

Quilt Top Assembly Diagram

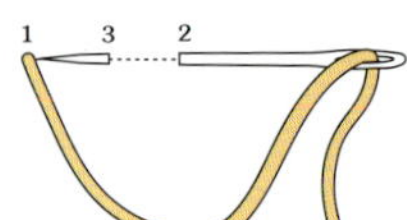

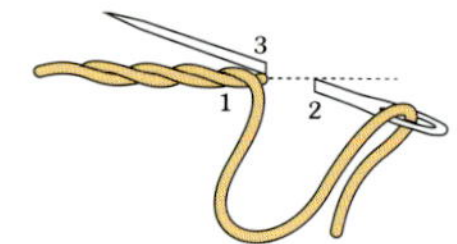

Stemstitch Diagram

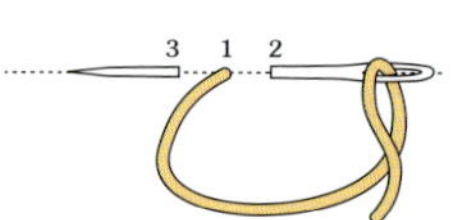

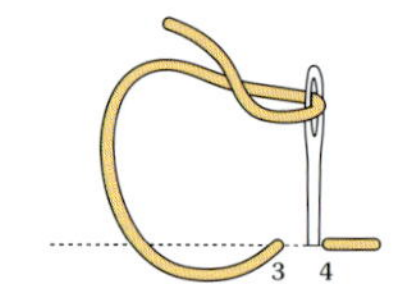

Backstitch Diagram

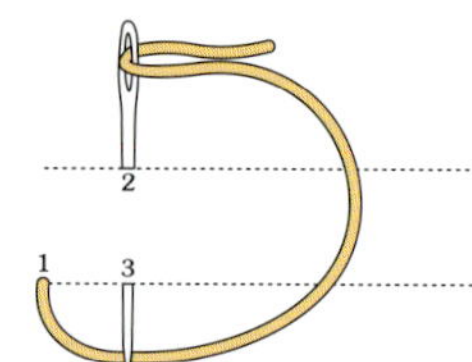

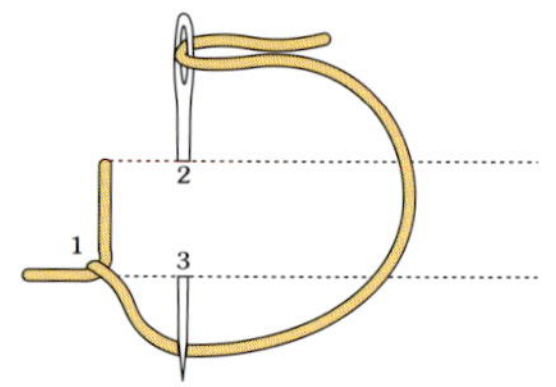

Buttonhole-Stitch Diagram

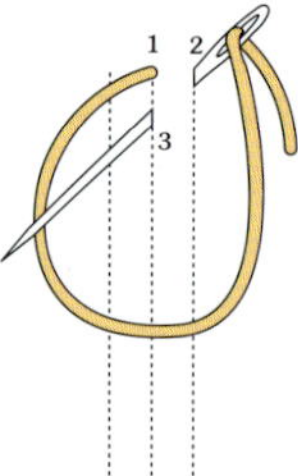

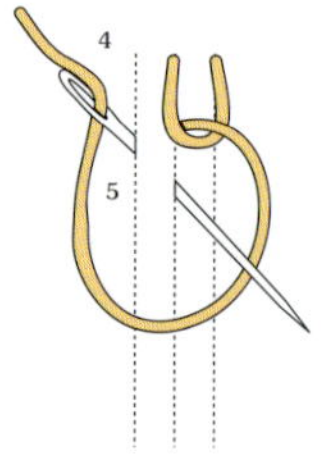

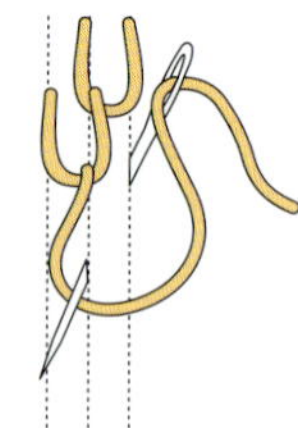

Feather-Stitch Diagram

Lost in the Cornfield has little touches of embroidery throughout for extra interest. Buttons are used to represent falling kernals below the occasional ripe ear of corn.

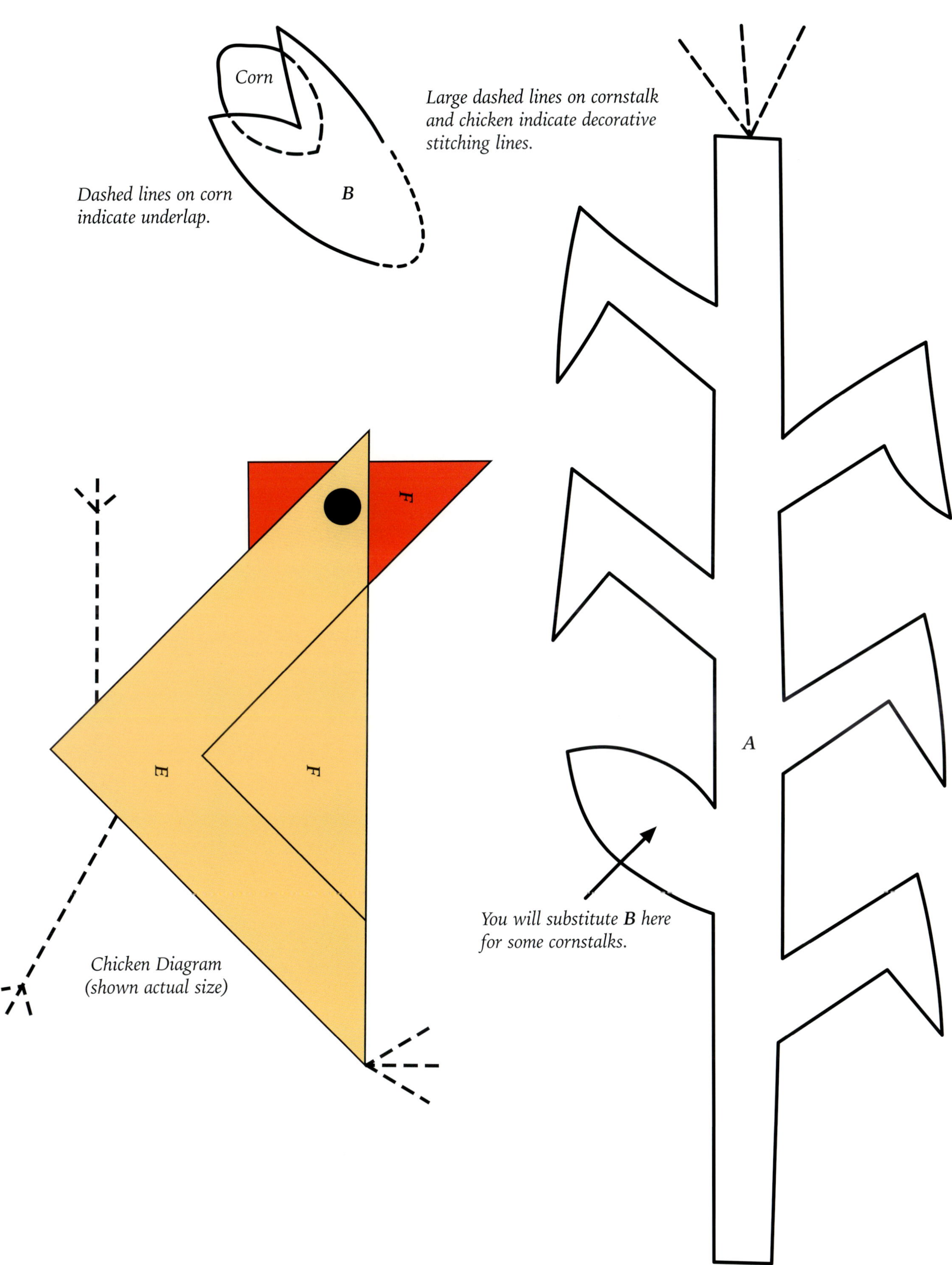

Chicken Diagram (shown actual size)

October

You'll have a ghoulishly good time *quilting this eerie-sistible wall hanging! The dimensional quilt features windows and doors that open to reveal ghouls and witches hiding inside. To make this quilt, you'll need a Halloween novelty print that has several different motifs. We used Grave Expectations by Alexander Henry.*

The House on Haunted Hill

Quilt designed and made by Cynthia Moody Wheeler

Finished Size: 32" x 34"

Materials

1/2 yd Halloween motif novelty print
2/3 yd blue print for sky
1/4 yd green print for grass
1/8 yd gold print for windows
1/4 yd red-and-black print for house
1/4 yd red print for inner border
1/8 yd black stripe for shutters and door
1/4 yd gray plaid for roof
5/8 yd black-and-white print for tree
2 yds light gray print for outer borders, backing, and binding
2 yds paper-backed fusible web
Thread: gray, black, blue, green, and red
1 yd tear-away stabilizer
1 yd batting

Cutting

From blue print, cut:
- 1 (19 1/2" x 22 1/2") rectangle for sky.

From green print, cut:
- 1 (5 1/2" x 22 1/2") rectangle for grass.

From red print, cut:
- 4 (1 1/2" x 24 1/2") strips for inner border.

From gray print, cut:
- 2 (4 1/2" x 26 1/2") strips for outer side borders.
- 2 (4 1/2" x 32 1/2") strips for outer top and bottom borders.
- 1 (36") square for backing.
- Set remaining fabric aside for binding.

From black stripe, cut:
- 1 (3 1/2" x 26") strip for shutters.
- 1 (5" x 6") piece for door.

Follow manufacturer's instructions to fuse web to wrong side of following fabrics and then cut pieces as indicated.

From red-and-black print, cut:
- 1 (7" x 14") strip for lower house.
- 1 (4" x 10") strip for upper house.

From gray plaid, cut:
- 1 (2 1/4" x 14 1/2") strip for Roof 1 (long, lower roof). Measure in 1 1/2" from each short end and cut at 45° angle (see photo).
- 1 (6 1/2") square. Cut square in half diagonally. Use 1 half for Roof 2 (lower pointed roof).
- 1 (7 1/2") square. Cut square in half diagonally. Use 1 half for Roof 3 (upper roof). Measure down 2 5/8" on both sides from tip of roof and then cut off to flatten (see photo).
- 2 (1/2" x 6 1/4") strips for porch posts.

From gold print, cut:
- 1 (2 1/2" x 4 1/2") piece for lower left window.
- 1 (2 1/2" x 3 1/2") piece for lower right window.
- 1 (2 1/2") square for upper left window.
- 1 (1 1/2" x 2 1/2") for upper right window.
- 1 (2" x 5 1/2") piece for door.

From black-and-white print:
- Trace tree pattern on pages 56 and 57 onto paper side of 9 1/2" x 19 1/2" piece of fusible web. Fuse web to 10" x 20" rectangle for tree. Cut out tree along drawn lines.

Assembly

1. Sew grass piece to sky piece. Press seams open.
2. Fuse paper-backed fusible web to wrong side of novelty print. Select figures to appear in windows and door and cut out along outline of characters. Overlap figures on windows and door; trim excess novelty print as needed. Do not fuse yet. Set aside.
3. To make shutters, cut 1 (1 1/2" x 25 1/2") piece of fusible web. Fuse to wrong side of shutter fabric, keeping 1 long edge of web 1/4" away from 1 long edge of material. Remove paper backing. Fold fabric in half lengthwise and fuse. Trim shutter piece to 1 1/2"-wide. *Note: Be sure to trim from raw edge, leaving folded edge of fabric intact for outer edge of shutters.* Cut fused shutter fabric into 6 (2 1/2"-long) shutters and 2 (4 1/2"-long) shutters. Set aside.
4. To make door, cut 1 (2 1/4" x 5 1/2") piece of fusible web. Fuse to wrong side of black stripe door fabric, keeping 1 long edge of web 1/4" away from 1 long edge of material. Remove paper backing. Fold fabric in half lengthwise and fuse. Trim door piece 2 1/4"-wide from raw edge. Cut door 5 1/2" long. Set aside.

5. Position bottom edge of lower house piece 3¼" above bottom edge of grass and 1½" from right side. Center Roof 1 on lower house, overlapping house by ¼". Position upper house ¼" from upper right corner of Roof 1, tucking bottom edge ¼" under Roof 1. Center Roof 3 on upper house, overlapping house ¼". If you have a character for rooftop, such as a cat on a fence as shown in photo, tuck bottom edge of character under top of roof. Fuse pieces in place.
6. Position right side of gold door opening 4¼" from right side of lower house so that bottom of door is even with bottom of lower house. Tuck raw edge of black stripe door ¼" under left edge of gold door opening. Fuse in place. Position character in doorway and fuse in place.
7. Position lower right window ¼" from right edge of lower house so that top of window is even with top of door. Tuck raw edges of shutters under both sides of window and fuse in place. Position character in window and fuse in place.
8. Position lower left window ¾" from left edge of lower house so that top of window is even with top of door. Tuck raw edges of shutters under both sides of window and fuse in place.
9. Position Roof 2 piece ¾" below lower edge of Roof 1 and ½" from right side of lower house. Position porch posts so that bottom edges are even with bottom of lower house, outer edges of posts are ½" from bottom corners of Roof 2, and top edges are tucked under Roof 2. Fuse pieces in place. (Note that right post is fused over lower right window.)
10. Center upper left window on upper house ¾" from left edge. Center right window ¼" from right edge. Tuck raw edges of shutters under both sides of windows and fuse in place. Position characters in windows and fuse in place.

11. Referring to photo, fuse tree in place, allowing branches to overlap house.
12. Fuse extra motifs in place around the house and tree, such as pumpkins, gravestones, ghost, owl, and broom as desired.
13. Place tear-away stabilizer behind quilt top. Satin stitch around all roofs and posts with gray thread. Satin stitch around house, windows, and doors with black thread.
14. Add red side borders to quilt top and then red top/bottom borders. Add gray print side borders and then top/bottom borders.

Quilting and Finishing

1. Layer backing, batting, and quilt top. Baste. Quilt as desired. Quilt shown has straight stitching around house, roofs, and tree; stipple quilting in the sky; a grass-shaped free-motion stitch in the grass; random loops in the red borders; and meander quilting in the gray borders.
2. Trim wall hanging to 32" x 34".
3. To add hanging sleeve to back, fold under 2 short ends and bottom edge ½". Pin long raw edge to quilt back. (Raw edge will be covered by binding.)
4. Make 144" of binding. Refer to *Attaching French-Fold Binding with Mitered Corners,* page 79, to add binding to quilt.

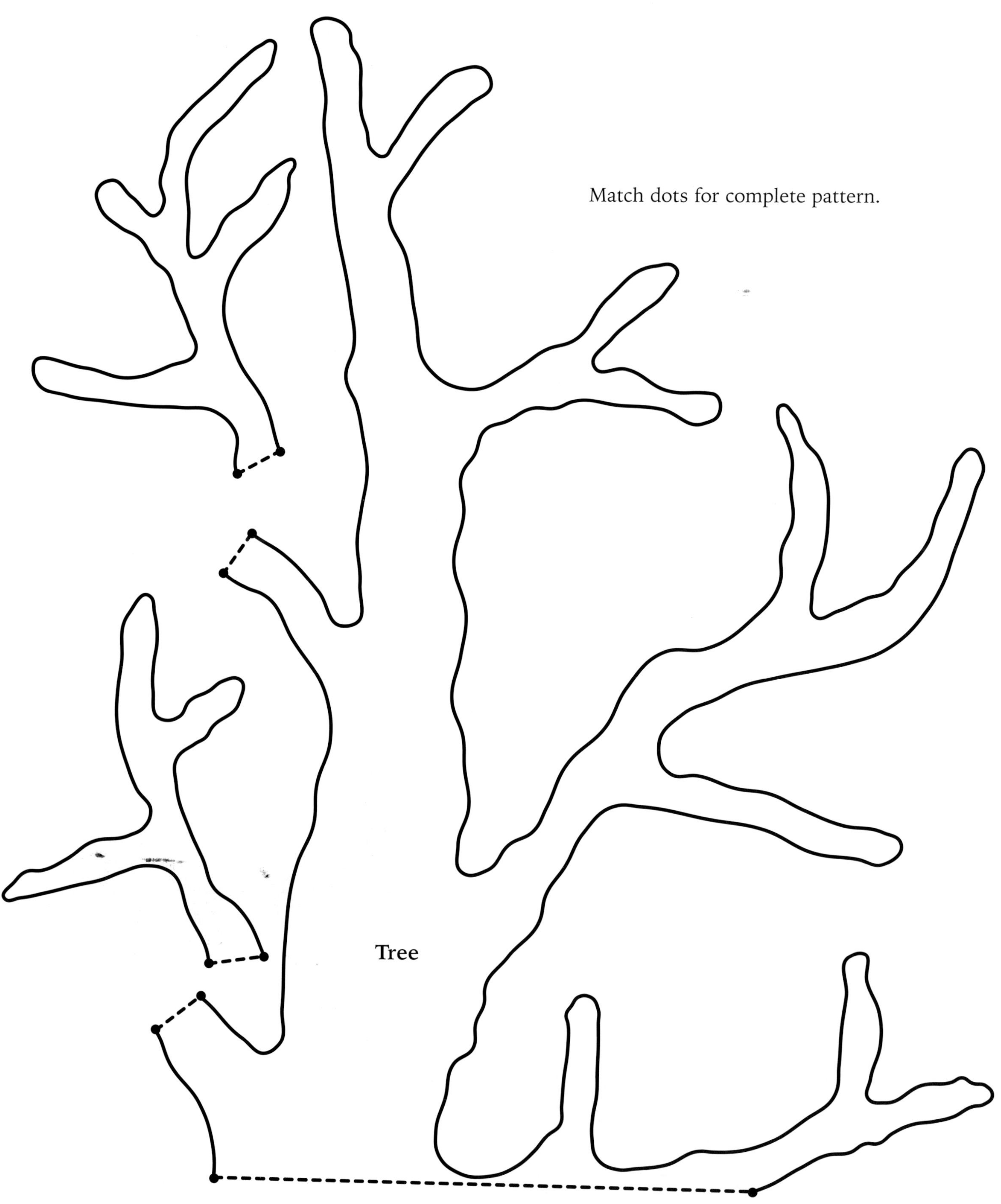
Match dots for complete pattern.
Tree

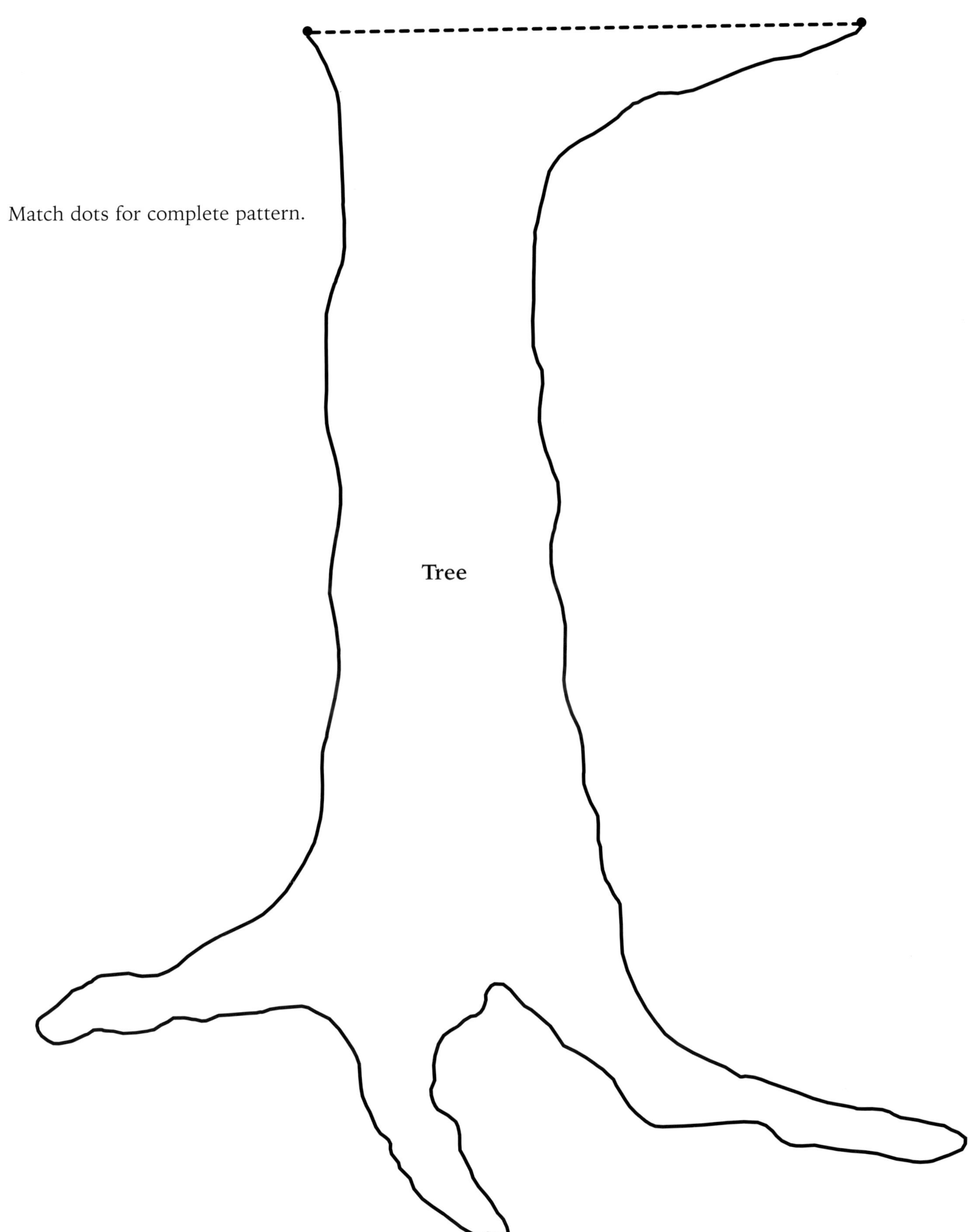
Match dots for complete pattern.
Tree

November

As summer gives way to autumn,

Mother Nature paints the leaves in a myriad of warm hues. Because this project uses a cornucopia of colors, it's a great way to use your scraps. Cover the guest bed with the old-fashioned quilt and your Thanksgiving company will have one more thing for which to be grateful.

Meg's Maple Leaves

Quilt by Meg McKinney Simle

Finished Size: 70" x 85"
Blocks: 12 (13") Maple Leaf Blocks

Materials

12 fat quarters* dark prints for leaves, pieced border, and sashing squares
12 fat quarters* light prints for block backgrounds
1 yd light tone-on-tone print for sashing strips
1 yd dark autumn print for inner borders (2 yds for unpieced borders)
1 yd medium autumn print for pieced border background
2½ yds dark brown print for outer border and binding
5 yds fabric for backing
Twin-size batting
Rotary cutter, mat, and acrylic ruler
*Fat quarter = 18" x 22"

Cutting

Measurements include ¼" seam allowances. Follow *Rotary Cutting*, page 71. Border strips are exact length needed, except for outer border, so that pieced borders will fit correctly.
From each dark fat quarter, cut:
- 4 sets of the following for leaves:
  - 4 (2½") B squares.
  - 2 (2⅞") squares. Cut squares in half diagonally to make 4 A triangles.
- 1 (1½") E square.
- 2 (2½") sashing squares.
- 8 (3") F squares for pieced border.

From each light fat quarter, cut:
- 4 (1½" x 6½") D block sashing strips.
- 4 sets of the following:
  - 1 (2½") B square for leaf background.
  - 2 (2⅞") squares. Cut squares in half diagonally to make 4 A triangles for leaf background.
  - 2 (2¼") C squares for stem unit.

From light tone-on-tone print, cut:
- 11 (2½"-wide) strips. Cut strips into 31 (2½" x 13½") sashing strips.

From dark autumn print, cut:
- 12 (2"-wide) strips. Piece to make 2 (2" x 62½") first inner side borders, 2 (2" x 50½") first inner top and bottom borders, 2 (2" x 70½") second inner side borders, and 2 (2" x 58½") second inner top and bottom borders. If you prefer unpieced borders, cut 8 (2"-wide) lengthwise strips from alternate yardage and trim to above lengths.

From medium autumn print, cut:
- 17 (1¾"-wide) strips. Cut strips into 384 (1¾") G squares for pieced border background. If you prefer, you may use several fabrics and/or scraps for pieced border block backgrounds.

From dark brown print, cut:
- 4 (6½"-wide) lengthwise strips the length of fabric for outer border.
- 4 (2¼"-wide) lengthwise strips the length of fabric for binding.

Block Assembly

1. Choose 1 set each dark and light leaf pieces. Join 1 light and 1 dark A triangle as shown in *Unit A Assembly Diagram* to make 1 A unit. Make 4 A units.

Unit A Assembly Diagram

2. Referring to *Stem Diagonal Seams Diagrams,* place 1 light C square atop 1 corner of 1 dark B square. Stitch diagonally from corner to corner of C square, trim excess fabric ¼" from stitching, and press open to reveal triangle. Repeat on opposite corner to make 1 stem unit.

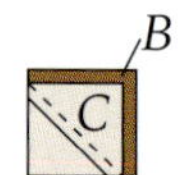

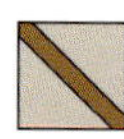

Stem Diagonal Seams Diagrams

3. Lay out A units, stem unit, and remaining matching B squares as shown in *Leaf Unit Assembly Diagram.* Join into rows; join rows to complete 1 leaf unit. Repeat to make 4 leaf units in assorted fabrics.

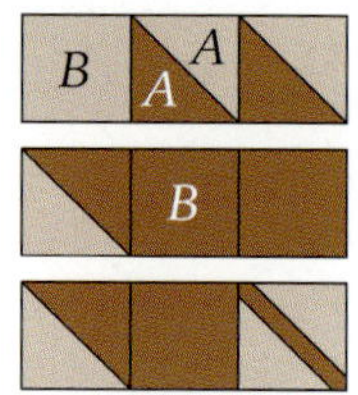

=

Leaf Unit Assembly Diagram

4. Referring to *Block Assembly Diagram,* lay out 4 leaf units with 4 ($1\frac{1}{2}$" x $6\frac{1}{2}$") D sashing strips and 1 dark E square. Mix or match as desired. Join into rows; join rows to complete 1 Maple Leaf block *(Block Diagram)*.
5. Make 12 Maple Leaf blocks.

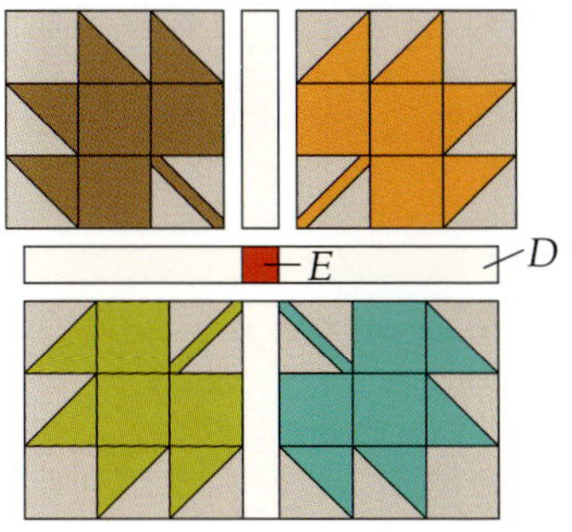
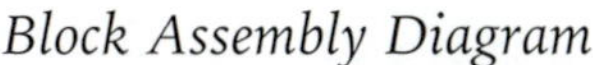

Block Assembly Diagram

Block Diagram

Border Assembly

1. Referring to *Border Diagonal Seams Diagrams,* place 1 G square atop 1 corner of 1 dark F square. Stitch diagonally from corner to corner, trim excess fabric $\frac{1}{4}$" from stitching, and press open to reveal triangle. Repeat on all 4 corners to make 1 border unit. Make 96 border units.

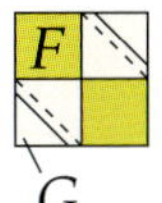

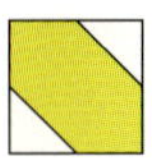
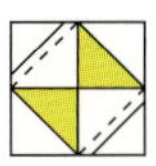
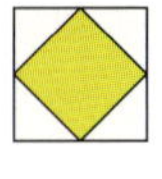

Border Diagonal Seams Diagrams

2. Join 26 border units to make 1 side border strip. Repeat. Join 22 border units to make 1 top border strip. Repeat for bottom border strip.

Just as diversity of color enhances the beauty of fall foliage, this quilt pattern is enriched by using a wide variety of autumn prints for the Maple Leaf blocks and the striking border.

Quilt Top Assembly Diagram

Quilt Assembly

1. Referring to *Quilt Top Assembly Diagram,* page 62, join 4 dark sashing squares and 3 light sashing strips to make 1 sashing row. Make 5 sashing rows.
2. Join 4 sashing strips and 3 Maple Leaf blocks to make 1 block row. Make 4 block rows.
3. Alternate sashing rows and block rows. Join rows.
4. Add 2" x 62½" dark autumn first inner side borders to quilt. Add 2" x 50½" top and bottom borders.
5. (For greater ease in measuring and cutting, our instructions and diagrams differ slightly from the original quilt in the number of border units used.) Add 1 (26-unit) pieced border strip to each side of quilt. Add 22-unit top and bottom pieced borders.
6. Add 2" x 70½" dark autumn second inner side borders. Add 2" x 58½" top and bottom borders.
7. Add 6½"-wide dark brown borders to quilt, centering on each side and beginning and ending seams **exactly** ¼" from each corner of quilt top. Backstitch at beginning and ending of stitching to reinforce. Fold one corner of quilt top diagonally with right sides together and matching edges. Use ruler to mark stitching line as shown in *Mitered Corner Diagram*. Sew on drawn line, backstitching at beginning and ending of stitching. Trim seam allowance to ¼" and press to one side. Repeat for other corners.

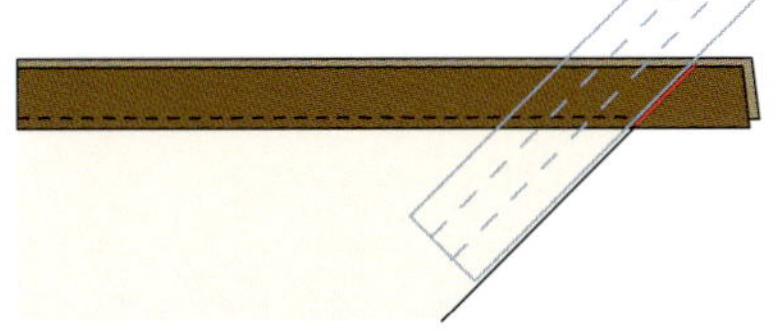

Mitered Corner Diagram

Quilting and Finishing

1. Divide backing fabric into 2 (2½-yd) lengths. Cut 1 piece in half lengthwise. Sew 1 narrow panel to each side of wide panel. Press seam allowances toward narrow panels.
2. Layer backing, batting, and quilt top; baste. Quilt as desired. Quilt shown was quilted in swirls in leaf blocks. Borders are outline-quilted. Large outer borders have straight-line quilting.
3. Join 2¼"-wide dark brown strips into 1 continuous piece for straight-grain binding. Refer to *Attaching French-Fold Binding with Mitered Corners,* page 79, to add binding to quilt.

Make A Pillow

To make a matching throw pillow, make one Maple Leaf block as described under *Block Assembly* on pages 60 and 61. Cut 2 (2½" x 13½") strips and 2 (2½" x 17½") strips from dark fabric. Join 13½" strips to opposite sides of the block and then join 17½"-long strips to the remaining sides of the block. Cut a 17½" square from a fall print for the backing. Layer the block and backing, with right sides facing. Sew ¼" from the outer edges, leaving a 4" opening for turning. Turn right side out, stuff with fiberfill, and slipstitch the opening closed.

December

As pretty as this quilt is,

you won't want to wait until the night before Christmas to get it out! The festive wrap is covered in Christmas stars to brighten the ambience of your home with holiday cheer. We quilted angel and garland motifs onto the wide outer border and then added straight-grain French-fold binding.

Christmas Stars

Design by Marsha McCloskey; published in On to Square Two *by* That Patchwork Place *in 1992; quilt shown by Nancy Graves*

Finished Size: 68" x 89"
Blocks: 35 (10$\frac{1}{2}$") Christmas Stars Blocks

Materials

12 fat quarters* light/medium neutral prints for block backgrounds
9 fat eights** assorted dark green prints #1 for star points and corners
12 fat eights** assorted dark red prints #1 for stars
1$\frac{1}{4}$ yds medium red print for blocks
3 yds dark red print #2 for blocks, border, and binding
$\frac{3}{4}$ yd dark green print #2 for border
$\frac{1}{2}$ yd tan print for border
5$\frac{1}{2}$ yds fabric for backing
Twin-size batting
Rotary cutter, cutting mat, and acrylic ruler
*Fat quarter = 18" x 22"
**Fat eighth = 9" x 22"

Cutting

Measurements include $\frac{1}{4}$" seam allowances. Cut crosswise strips unless otherwise noted. Follow *Rotary Cutting*, page 71. Border strips are exact length needed. You may want to cut them longer to allow for piecing variations.

From each fat eighth of light/medium neutral print, cut:

- 3 sets of:
  - 4 (3") C squares.
  - 2 (3$\frac{3}{8}$") squares. Cut squares in half diagonally to make 4 B triangles.
  - 1 (3$\frac{3}{4}$") square. Cut square in quarters diagonally to make 4 A triangles.

From each fat eighth of assorted dark green prints #1, cut:

- 4 sets of:
  - 2 (3$\frac{3}{8}$") squares. Cut squares in half diagonally to make 4 B triangles.
  - 1 (3$\frac{3}{4}$") square. Cut square in quarters diagonally to make 4 A triangles.

From each fat eighth of assorted dark red prints #1, cut:

- 3 sets of:
  - 2 (3$\frac{3}{8}$") squares. Cut squares in half diagonally to make 4 B triangles.
  - 1 (3") C square.

From medium red print, cut:

- 6 (6$\frac{1}{4}$"-wide) strips. Cut strips into 34 (6$\frac{1}{4}$") squares. Cut squares in half diagonally to make 68 D triangles for 17 blocks.

From dark red print #2, cut:

- 6 (6$\frac{1}{4}$"-wide) strips. Cut strips into 36 (6$\frac{1}{4}$") squares. Cut squares in half diagonally to make 72 D triangles for 18 blocks.
- 8 (5"-wide) strips. Join strips into 2 (5" x 80$\frac{1}{2}$") side borders and 2 (5" x 68$\frac{1}{2}$") top and bottom borders.
- 9 (2$\frac{1}{4}$"-wide) strips for binding.

From dark green print #2, cut:

- 7 (2$\frac{1}{2}$"-wide) strips. Piece strips to make 2 (2$\frac{1}{2}$" x 74") side borders and 2 (2$\frac{1}{2}$" x 57") top and bottom borders.

From tan print, cut:

- 7 (1$\frac{3}{4}$"-wide) strips. Piece strips to make 2 (1$\frac{3}{4}$" x 78") side borders and 2 (1$\frac{3}{4}$" x 59$\frac{1}{2}$") top and bottom borders.

Block Assembly

1. Choose 1 set each of green (4 As, 4 Bs), light/medium neutrals (4 As, 4 Cs, 4 Bs), and dark red #1 pieces (4 Bs, 1 C), plus 4 matching medium red or dark red #2 D triangles.
2. Join 1 green and 1 neutral A triangle as shown in *Star Point Assembly Diagrams*. Join to 1 red B triangle to make 1 point unit. Make 4 point units.

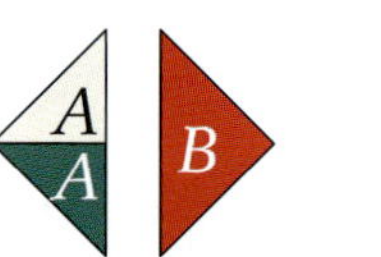

Star Point Assembly Diagrams

3. Lay out 1 red C, 4 neutral Cs, and 4 point units as shown in *Star Assembly Diagram*. Join into rows; join rows to complete star center.

Star Assembly Diagram

4. Join 1 green and 1 neutral B triangle as shown in *Corner Triangle Assembly Diagrams* to make 1 square. Place square on corner of D triangle. (Pay careful attention to color and seam placement.) Using diagonal seams, stitch diagonally across square. Trim and open out to make 1 corner unit. Make 4 corner units.

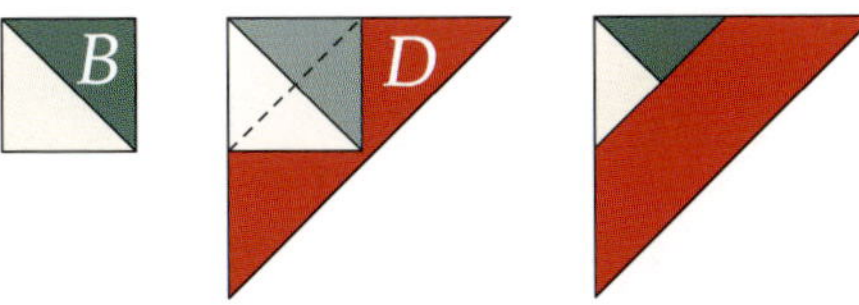

Corner Triangle Assembly Diagrams

5. Add 1 corner unit to each side of star center as shown in *Block Assembly Diagram* to complete 1 Christmas Star block. Trim block to 11" to 11."
6. Make 35 Christmas Star blocks *(Block Diagram)*, 17 with medium red D triangles and 18 with dark red D triangles.

Block Assembly Diagram

Block Diagram

Quilt Assembly

1. Lay out blocks as shown in *Quilt Top Assembly Diagram,* alternating dark red and medium red blocks. Join into rows; join rows to complete center.
2. Add green side borders to quilt. Add top and bottom borders.
3. Add tan side borders to quilt. Add top and bottom borders.
4. Add red side borders to quilt. Add top and bottom borders.

Quilting and Finishing

1. Divide backing fabric into 2 (2¾-yd) lengths. Cut 1 piece in half lengthwise. Sew 1 narrow panel to each side of wide panel. Press seam allowances toward narrow panels.
2. Layer backing, batting, and quilt top; baste. Quilt as desired. Quilt shown has outline quilting on patchwork, with star points on block backgrounds and hearts in block centers. Red E triangles have 3 parallel lines quilted through them, which extend into green and tan borders. Outer border has angel and garland motifs.
3. Join 2¼"-wide dark red strips into 1 continuous piece for straight-grain binding. Refer to *Attaching French-Fold Binding with Mitered Corners,* page 79, to add binding to quilt.

Quilt Top Assembly Diagram

Start a New Tradition

Nancy Graves made this quilt for her entire family to share during the holidays. Each one takes a turn sleeping under it between Thanksgiving and Christmas. "I make a new label every year, and each person signs it—even our dog, Scooby," says Nancy. "We've been doing it for about seven years. My father-in-law and grandmother have died since we've started the tradition, so it is becoming more special to us." *Christmas Stars* won Best of Show at the Kansas State Fair in 1995.

GENERAL INSTRUCTIONS

Complete instructions are given for making each of the quilts shown in this book. To make your quilting easier and more enjoyable, we encourage you to carefully read all of the general instructions, study the color photographs, and familiarize yourself with the individual project instructions before beginning a project.

QUILTING SUPPLIES

This list includes all the tools you need for basic quick-method quiltmaking, plus additional supplies used for special techniques. Unless otherwise specified, all items may be found in your favorite fabric store or quilt shop.

Batting — Batting is most commonly available in polyester, cotton, or a polyester/cotton blend (see **Choosing and Preparing the Batting**, page 76).

Cutting mat — A cutting mat is a special mat designed to be used with a rotary cutter. A mat that measures approximately 18" x 24" is a good size for most cutting.

Eraser — A soft white fabric eraser or white art eraser may be used to remove pencil marks from fabric. Do not use a colored eraser, as the dye may discolor fabric.

Iron — An iron with both steam and dry settings and a smooth, clean soleplate is necessary for proper pressing.

Marking tools — There are many different marking tools available (see **Marking Quilting Lines**, page 76). A silver quilter's pencil is a good marker for both light and dark fabrics.

Masking tape — Two widths of masking tape, 1"-wide and 1/4"-wide, are helpful when quilting. The 1"-wide tape is used to secure the backing fabric to a flat surface when layering the quilt. The 1/4"-wide tape may be used as a guide when outline quilting.

Needles — Two types of needles are used for hand sewing: Betweens, used for quilting, are short and strong for stitching through layered fabric and batting. Sharps are longer, thinner needles used for basting and other hand sewing. For sewing machine needles, we recommend size 10 to 14 or 70 to 90 universal (sharp-pointed) needles.

Permanent fine-point pen — A permanent pen is used to mark templates and stencils and to sign and date quilts. Test pen on fabric to make sure it will not bleed or wash out.

Pins — Straight pins made especially for quilting are extra long with large round heads. Glass head pins will stand up to occasional contact with a hot iron. Some quilters prefer extra-fine dressmaker's silk pins. If you are machine quilting, you will need a large supply of 1" long (size 01) rustproof safety pins for pin-basting.

Quilting hoop or frame — Quilting hoops and frames are designed to hold the 3 layers of a quilt together securely while you quilt. Many different types and sizes are available, including round and oval wooden hoops, frames made of rigid plastic pipe, and large floor frames made of either material. A 14" or 16" hoop allows you to quilt in your lap and makes your quilting portable.

Rotary cutter — The rotary cutter is the essential tool for quick-method quilting techniques. The cutter consists of a round, sharp blade mounted on a handle with a retractable blade guard for safety. It should be used only with a cutting mat and rotary cutting ruler. Three sizes are generally available; we recommend the 45 mm size.

Rotary cutting ruler — A rotary cutting ruler is a thick, clear acrylic ruler made specifically for use with a rotary cutter. It should have accurate 1/8" crosswise and lengthwise markings and markings for 45° and 60° angles. A 6" x 24" ruler is a good size for most cutting. An additional 12 1/2" square ruler is helpful when cutting wider pieces. Many specialty rulers are available that make specific cutting tasks faster and easier.

Scissors — Although most fabric cutting will be done with a rotary cutter, sharp, high-quality scissors are still needed for some cutting. A separate pair of scissors for cutting paper and plastic is recommended. Smaller scissors are handy for clipping threads.

Seam ripper — A good seam ripper with a fine point is useful for removing stitching.

Sewing machine — A sewing machine that produces a good, even straight stitch is all that is necessary for most quilting. Clean and oil your machine often and keep the tension set properly.

Tape measure — A flexible 120" long tape measure is helpful for measuring a quilt top before adding borders.

Template material — Sheets of translucent plastic, often pre-marked with a grid, are made especially for making quilting stencils.

Thimble — A thimble is necessary when hand quilting. Thimbles are available in metal, plastic, or leather and in many sizes and styles. Choose a thimble that fits well and is comfortable.

Thread — Several types of thread are used for quiltmaking: *General-purpose* sewing thread is used for basting and piecing. Choose high-quality cotton or cotton-covered polyester thread in light and dark neutrals, such as ecru and grey, for your basic supplies. *Quilting* thread is stronger than general-purpose sewing thread, and some brands have a coating to make them slide more easily through the quilt layers.

Triangle — A large plastic right-angle triangle (available in art and office supply stores) is useful in rotary cutting for making first cuts to "square up" raw edges of fabric and for checking to see that cuts remain at right angles to the fold.

Walking foot — A walking foot, or even-feed foot, is needed for straight-line machine quilting. This special foot will help all 3 layers move at the same rate over the feed dogs to provide a smoother quilted project. Use your walking foot when stitching binding to your quilt.

FABRICS

SELECTING FABRICS

Choose high-quality, medium-weight 100% cotton fabrics such as broadcloth or calico. All-cotton fabrics hold a crease better, fray less, and are easier to quilt than cotton/polyester blends. All the fabrics for a quilt should be of comparable weight and weave. Check the end of the fabric bolt for fiber content and width.

The yardage requirements listed for each project are based on 45" wide fabric with a "usable" width of 42" after shrinkage and trimming selvages. Your actual usable width will probably vary slightly from fabric to fabric. Though most fabrics will yield 42" or more, if you find a fabric that you suspect will yield a narrower usable width, you will need to purchase additional yardage to compensate. Our recommended yardage lengths should be adequate for occasional resquaring of fabric when many cuts are required, but it never hurts to buy a little more fabric for insurance against a narrower usable width, the occasional cutting error, or to have on hand for making coordinating projects.

PREPARING FABRICS

All fabrics should be washed, dried, and pressed before cutting.

1. To check colorfastness before washing, cut a small piece of the fabric and place in a glass of hot water with a little detergent. Leave fabric in the water for a few minutes. Remove fabric from water and blot with white paper towels. If any color bleeds onto the towels, wash the fabric separately with warm water and detergent, then rinse until the water runs clear. If fabric continues to bleed, choose another fabric.
2. Unfold yardage and separate fabrics by color. To help reduce raveling, use scissors to snip a small triangle from each corner of your fabric pieces. Machine wash fabrics in warm water with a small amount of mild laundry detergent. Do not use fabric softener. Rinse well and then dry fabrics in the dryer, checking long fabric lengths occasionally to make sure they are not tangling.
3. To make ironing easier, remove fabrics from dryer while they are slightly damp. Refold each fabric lengthwise (as it was on the bolt) with wrong sides together and matching selvages. If necessary, adjust slightly at selvages so that fold lays flat. Press each fabric using a steam iron set on "cotton."

ROTARY CUTTING

Based on the idea that you can easily cut strips of fabric and then cut those strips into smaller pieces, rotary cutting has brought speed and accuracy to quiltmaking. Observe safety precautions when using the rotary cutter, since it is extremely sharp. Develop a habit of retracting the blade guard ***just before*** *making a cut and closing it* ***immediately afterward,*** *before laying down the cutter.*

1. Follow **Preparing Fabrics**, page 70, to wash, dry, and press fabrics.
2. Cut all strips from the selvage-to-selvage width of the fabric unless otherwise indicated in project instructions. Place fabric on the cutting mat, as shown in *Fig. 1,* with the fold of the fabric toward you. To straighten the uneven fabric edge, make the first "squaring up" cut by placing the right edge of the rotary cutting ruler over the left raw edge of the fabric. Place right-angle triangle (or another rotary cutting ruler) with the lower edge carefully aligned with the fold and the left edge against the ruler *(Fig. 2)*. Hold the ruler firmly with your left hand, placing your little finger off the left edge to anchor the ruler. Remove the triangle, pick up the rotary cutter, and retract the blade guard. Using a smooth downward motion, make the cut by running the blade of the rotary cutter firmly along the right edge of the ruler *(Fig. 2)*. **Always** cut in a direction **away** from your body and **immediately** close the blade guard after each cut.

Fig. 1

Fig. 2

3. To cut each of the strips required for a project, place the ruler over the cut edge of the fabric, aligning desired marking on the ruler with the cut edge *(Fig. 3);* make the cut. When cutting several strips from a single piece of fabric, it is important to occasionally use the ruler and triangle to ensure that cuts are still at a perfect right angle to the fold. If not, repeat Step 2 to straighten.

Fig. 3

4. To square up selvage ends of a strip before cutting pieces, refer to *Fig. 4* and place folded strip on mat with selvage ends to your right. Aligning a horizontal marking on ruler with 1 long edge of strip, use rotary cutter to trim selvage to make end of strip square and even *(Fig. 4)*. Turn strip (or entire mat) so that cut end is to your left before making subsequent cuts.

Fig. 4

5. Pieces such as rectangles and squares can now be cut from strips. Usually strips remain folded, and pieces are cut in pairs after ends of strips are squared up. To cut squares or rectangles from a strip, place ruler over left end of strip, aligning desired marking on ruler with cut end of strip. To ensure perfectly square cuts, align a horizontal marking on ruler with 1 long edge of strip *(Fig. 5)* before making the cut.

Fig. 5

6. To cut 2 triangles from a square, cut square the size indicated in the project instructions. Cut square once diagonally to make 2 triangles *(Fig. 6)*.

Fig. 6

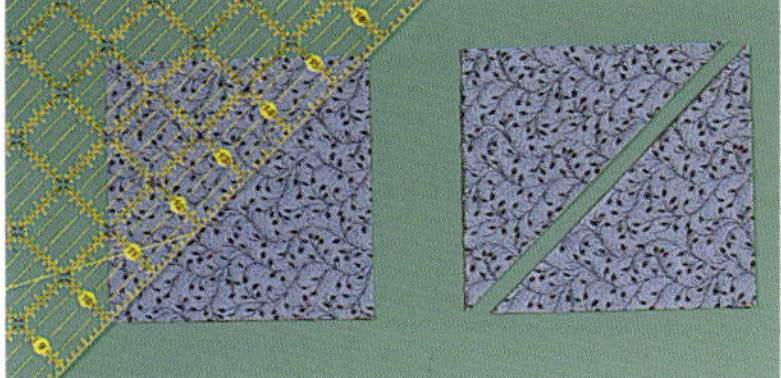

7. To cut 4 triangles from a square, cut square the size indicated in the project instructions. Cut square twice diagonally to make 4 triangles *(Fig. 7)*. You may find it helpful to use a small rotary cutting mat so that the mat can be turned to make second cut without disturbing fabric pieces.

Fig. 7

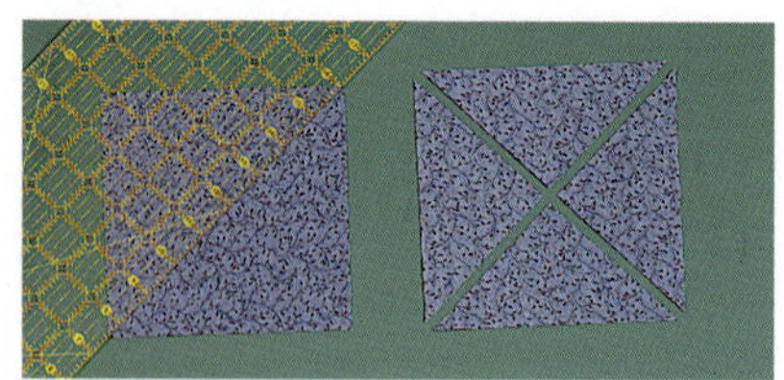

8. After some practice, you may want to try stacking up to 6 fabric layers when making cuts. When stacking strips, match long cut edges and follow Step 4 to square up ends of strip stack. Carefully turn stack (or entire mat) so that squared-up ends are to your left before making subsequent cuts. After cutting, check accuracy of pieces. Some shapes, such as diamonds, are more difficult to cut accurately in stacks.
9. In some cases, strips will be sewn together into strip sets before being cut into smaller units. When cutting a strip set, align a seam in strip set with a horizontal marking on the ruler to maintain square cuts *(Fig. 8)*.

Fig. 8

PIECING AND PRESSING

Precise cutting, followed by accurate piecing and careful pressing, will ensure that all the pieces of your quilt top fit together well.

PIECING

Set sewing machine stitch length for approximately 11 stitches per inch. Use a new, sharp needle suited for medium-weight woven fabric. Use a neutral-colored general-purpose sewing thread (not quilting thread) in the needle and in the bobbin. Stitch first on a scrap of fabric to check upper and bobbin thread tension; make any adjustments necessary.

For good results, it is **essential** that you stitch with an **accurate 1/4" seam allowance**. On many sewing machines, the measurement from the needle to the outer edge of the presser foot is 1/4". If this is the case with your machine, the presser foot is your best guide. If not, measure 1/4" from the needle and mark throat plate with a piece of masking tape. Special presser feet that are exactly 1/4" wide are also available for most sewing machines.

When piecing, **always** place pieces **right sides together** and **match raw edges**; pin if necessary. (If using straight pins, remove the pins just before they reach the sewing machine needle.)

Chain Piecing

Chain piecing whenever possible will make your work go faster and will usually result in more accurate piecing. Stack the pieces you will be sewing beside your machine in the order you will need them and in a position that will allow you to easily pick them up. Pick up each pair of pieces, carefully place them together as they will be sewn, and feed them into the machine one after the other. Stop between each pair only long enough to pick up the next pair; don't cut thread between pairs *(Fig. 9)*. After all pieces are sewn, cut threads, press, and go on to the next step, chain piecing when possible.

Fig. 9

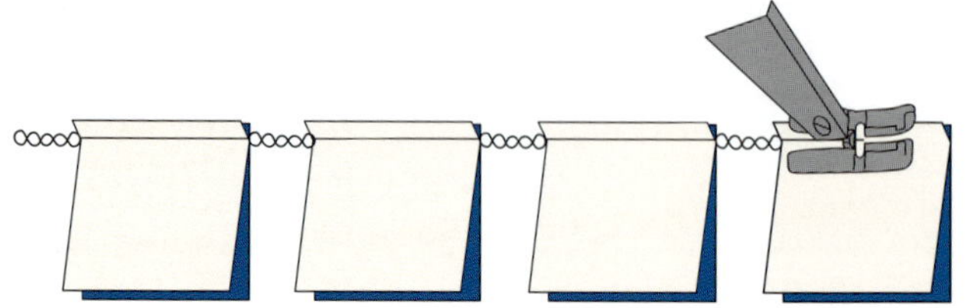

Sewing Strip Sets

When there are several strips to assemble into a strip set, first sew the strips together into pairs, then sew the pairs together to form the strip set. To help avoid distortion, sew 1 seam in 1 direction and then sew the next seam in the opposite direction *(Fig. 10)*.

Fig. 10

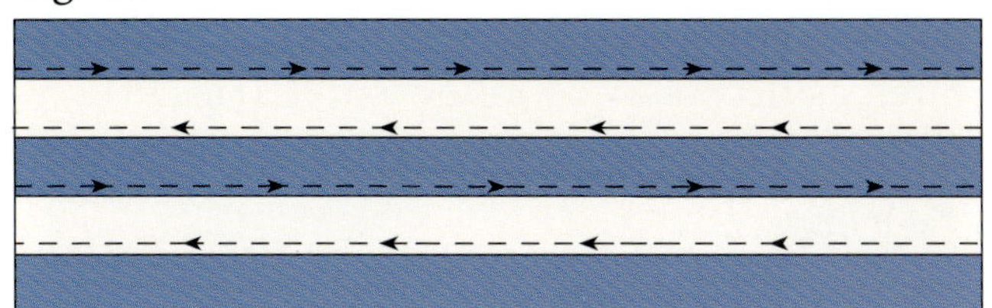

Sewing Across Seam Intersections

When sewing across the intersection of 2 seams, place pieces right sides together and match seams exactly, making sure seam allowances are pressed in opposite directions *(Fig. 11)*.

Fig. 11

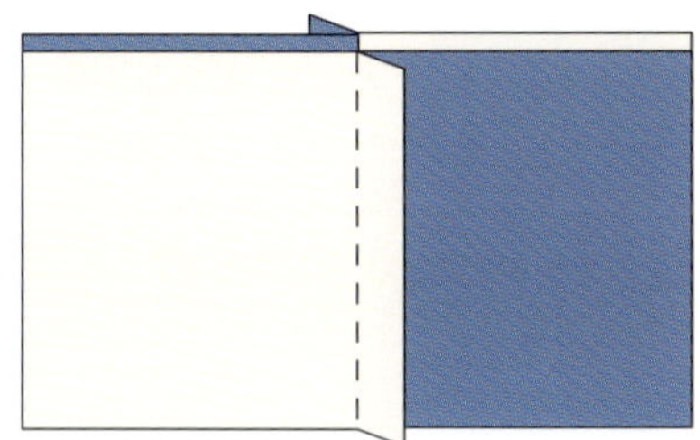

Sewing Bias Seams

Care should be used in handling and stitching bias edges since they stretch easily. After sewing the seam, carefully press seam allowance to 1 side, making sure not to stretch fabric.

Sewing Sharp Points

To ensure sharp points when joining triangular or diagonal pieces, stitch across the center of the "X" (shown in pink) formed on the wrong side by previous seams *(Fig. 12)*.

Fig. 12

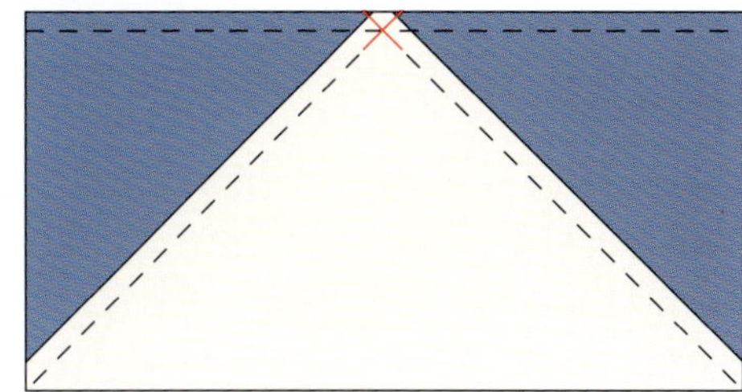

Trimming Seam Allowances

When sewing with triangle pieces, some seam allowances may extend beyond the edges of the sewn pieces. Trim away "dog ears" that extend beyond the edges of the sewn pieces *(Fig. 13)*.

Fig. 13

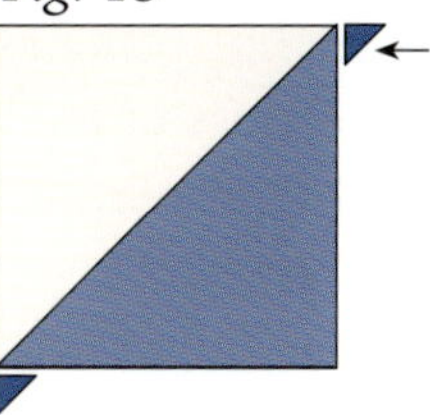

Pressing

Use a steam iron set on "cotton" for all pressing. Press as you sew, taking care to prevent small folds along seamlines. Seam allowances are almost always pressed to one side, usually toward the darker fabric. However, to reduce bulk it may occasionally be necessary to press seam allowances toward the lighter fabric or even to press them open. In order to prevent a dark fabric seam allowance from showing through a light fabric, trim the darker seam allowance slightly narrower than the lighter seam allowance. To press long seams, such as those in long strip sets, without curving or other distortion, lay strips across the width of the ironing board.

APPLIQUÉ

SATIN STITCH APPLIQUÉING

A good satin stitch is a thick, smooth, almost solid line of zigzag stitching that covers the exposed raw edges of appliqué pieces.

1. Place a stabilizer, such as paper or any of the commercially available products, on wrong side of background fabric before stitching appliqués in place.
2. Thread needle of sewing machine with general-purpose thread. Use thread that matches the background fabric in the bobbin for all stitching. Set sewing machine for a medium width zigzag stitch (approximately 1/8") and a very short stitch length. Set upper tension slightly looser than for regular stitching.
3. Beginning on as straight an edge as possible, position fabric so that most of the satin stitch will be on the appliqué piece. Do not backstitch; hold upper thread toward you and sew over it two or three stitches to anchor thread. Following Steps 4–7 for stitching corners and curves, stitch over exposed raw edges of appliqué pieces, changing thread color as necessary.
4. *(Note: Dots on Figs. indicate where to leave needle in fabric when pivoting.)* For outside corners, stitch 1/8" past the corner, stopping with the needle in background fabric *(Fig. 14)*. Raise presser foot. Pivot project, lower presser foot, and stitch adjacent side *(Fig. 15)*.

Fig. 14 *Fig. 15*

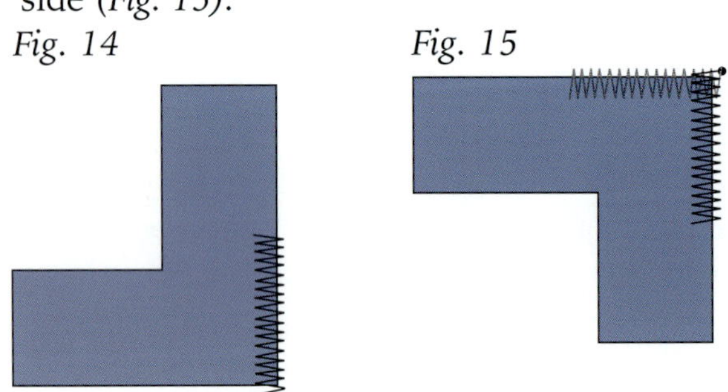

5. For inside corners, stitch 1/8" past the corner, stopping with the needle in the appliqué fabric *(Fig. 16)*. Raise presser foot. Pivot project, lower presser foot, and stitch adjacent side *(Fig. 17)*.

Fig. 16 *Fig. 17*

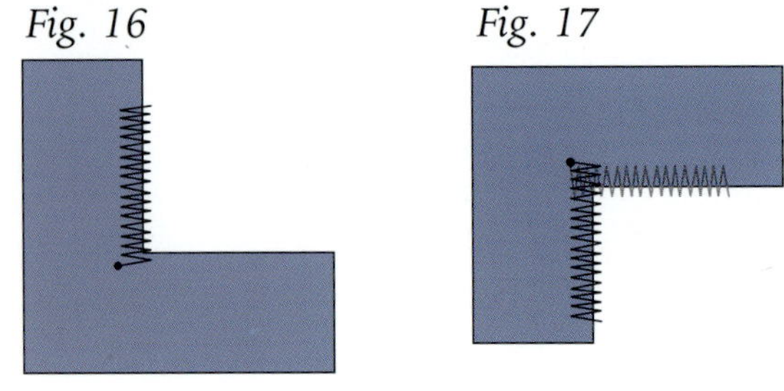

6. When stitching outside curves, stop with needle in background fabric. Raise presser foot and pivot project as needed. Lower presser foot and continue stitching, pivoting as often as necessary to follow curve *(Fig. 18)*. When stitching inside curves, stop with needle in appliqué fabric. Raise presser foot and pivot project as needed. Lower presser foot and continue stitching, pivoting as often as necessary to follow curve *(Fig. 19)*.

Fig. 18

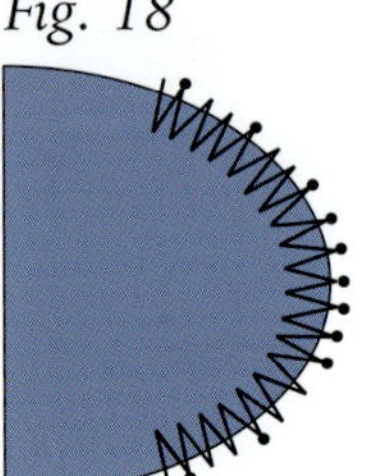

Fig. 19

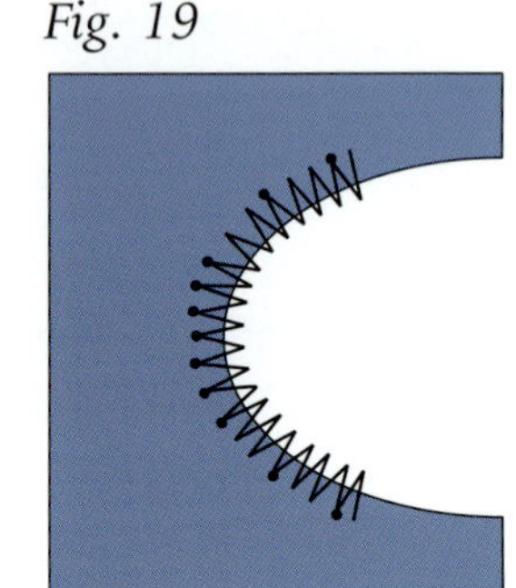

7. Do not backstitch at end of stitching. Pull threads to wrong side of background fabric; knot thread and trim ends. Remove paper and stabilizer.

HAND APPLIQUÉ

In this traditional hand appliqué method, the needle is used to turn the seam allowance under as you sew the appliqué to the background fabric using a blind stitch, page 79.

1. Place template on right side of appliqué fabric. Use a pencil to lightly draw around template, leaving at least 1/2" between shapes; repeat for number of shapes specified in project instructions.
2. Cut out shapes approximately 3/16" outside drawn line. Clip inside curves and points up to, but not through, drawn line. Arrange shapes on background fabric and pin or baste in place.
3. Thread a "sharps" needle with a single strand of general purpose sewing thread; knot one end.
4. For each appliqué shape, begin on as straight an edge as possible and turn a small section of seam allowance to wrong side with needle, concealing drawn line. Use blind stitch to sew appliqué to background, turning under edge and stitching as you continue around shape. Do not turn under or stitch seam allowances that will be covered by other appliqué pieces.
5. Follow **Cutting Away Fabric From Behind Appliqués**, page 75, to reduce bulk behind appliqués.

CUTTING AWAY FABRIC FROM BEHIND APPLIQUÉS

Hand quilting an appliquéd block will be easier if you are stitching through as few layers as possible. For this reason, or just to reduce bulk in your quilt, you may wish to cut away the background fabric behind appliqués. After stitching appliqués in place, turn block over and use sharp scissors or specially-designed appliqué scissors to trim away background fabric approximately 3/16" from stitching line. Take care not to cut appliqué fabric or stitches.

QUILTING

*Quilting holds the 3 layers (top, batting, and backing) of the quilt together and can be done by hand or machine. Because marking, layering, and quilting are interrelated and may be done in different orders depending on circumstances, please read the entire **Quilting** section, pages 75 - 78, before beginning the quilting process on your project.*

TYPES OF QUILTING

In the Ditch

Quilting very close to a seamline *(Fig. 20)* or appliqué *(Fig. 21)* is called "in the ditch" quilting. This type of quilting does not need to be marked. When quilting in the ditch, quilt on the side **opposite** the seam allowance.

Fig. 20

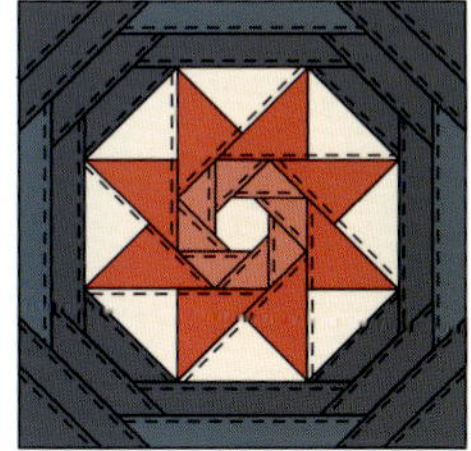

Fig. 21

Outline Quilting

Quilting approximately 1/4" from a seam or appliqué is called "outline" quilting *(Fig. 22)*. Outline quilting may be marked, or you may place 1/4"-wide masking tape along seamlines and quilt along the opposite edge of the tape. (Do not leave tape on quilt longer than necessary, since it may leave an adhesive residue.)

Fig. 22

Ornamental Quilting

Quilting decorative lines or designs is called "ornamental" quilting *(Fig. 23)*. This type of quilting should be marked before you baste quilt layers together.

Fig. 23

Machine Stipple Quilting

The term, "stipple quilting," refers to dense quilting using a meandering line of machine stitching or closely spaced hand stitching.

1. Wind your sewing machine bobbin with general-purpose thread that matches the quilt backing. Do not use quilting thread. Thread the needle of your machine with transparent monofilament thread if you want your quilting to blend with your quilt top fabrics. Use decorative thread, such as a metallic or contrasting-colored general-purpose thread, when you want the quilting lines to stand out more.
2. For random stipple quilting, use a darning foot, drop or cover feed dogs, and set stitch length at zero. Pull up bobbin thread and hold both thread ends while you stitch 2 or 3 stitches in place to lock thread. Cut threads near quilt surface. Place hands lightly on quilt on either side of darning foot.
3. Begin stitching in a meandering pattern *(Fig. 24)*, guiding the quilt with your hands. The object is to make stitches of similar length and to not sew over previous stitching lines. The movement of your hands is what determines the stitch length; it takes practice to coordinate your hand motions and the pressure you put on the foot pedal, so go slowly and practice at first.

Fig. 24

4. Continue machine quilting, filling in one open area of the quilt before moving on to another area, locking thread again at end of each line of stitching by sewing 2 or 3 stitches in place and trimming thread ends.

MARKING QUILTING LINES

Fabric marking pencils and various types of chalk markers are readily available and work well for different applications. Lead pencils work well on light-color fabrics, but marks may be difficult to remove. White pencils work well on dark-color fabrics, and silver pencils show up well on many colors. Since chalk rubs off easily, it's a good choice if you are marking as you quilt. Fabric marking pens make more durable and visible markings, but the marks should be carefully removed according to manufacturer's instructions. Press down only as hard as necessary to make a visible line when using all markers.

When you choose to mark your quilt, whether before or after the layers are basted together, is also a factor in deciding which marking tool to use. If you mark with chalk or a chalk pencil, handling the quilt during basting may rub off the markings. Intricate or ornamental designs may not be practical to mark as you quilt; mark these designs before basting using a more durable marker.

To choose marking tools, take all these factors into consideration and **test** different markers **on scrap fabric** until you find the one that gives the desired result.

USING QUILTING STENCILS

A wide variety of precut quilting stencils, as well as entire books of quilting patterns, are available. Using a stencil makes it easier to mark intricate or repetitive designs on your quilt top.

1. To make a stencil from a pattern, center template plastic over pattern and use a permanent marker to trace pattern onto plastic.
2. Use a craft knife with a single or double blade to cut narrow slits along traced lines *(Fig. 25)*.

Fig. 25

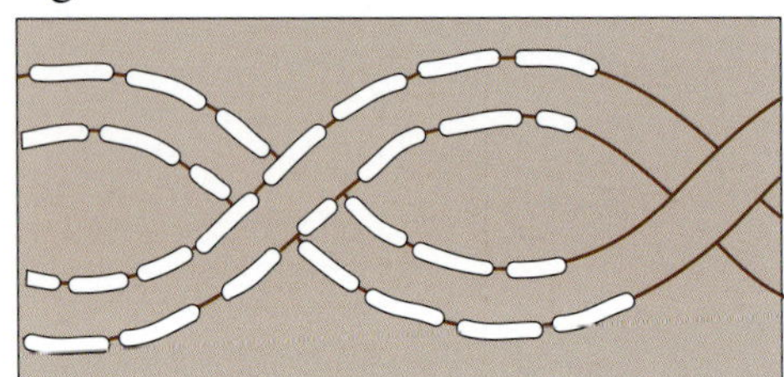

3. Use desired marking tool and stencil to mark quilting lines.

CHOOSING AND PREPARING THE BATTING

Choosing the right batting will make your quilting job easier. For fine hand quilting, choose a low-loft batting in any of the fiber types described here. Machine quilters will want to choose a low-loft batting that is all cotton or a cotton/polyester blend because the cotton helps "grip" the layers of the quilt. If the quilt is to be tied, a high-loft batting, sometimes called extra-loft or fat batting, is a good choice.

Batting is available in many different fibers. Bonded polyester batting is one of the most popular batting types. It is treated with a protective coating to stabilize the fibers and to reduce "bearding," a process in which batting fibers work their way out through the quilt fabrics. Other batting options include cotton/polyester batting, which combines the best of both polyester and cotton battings; all-cotton batting, which must be quilted more closely than polyester batting; and wool and silk battings, which are generally more expensive and usually only dry-cleanable.

Whichever batting you choose, read the manufacturer's instructions closely for any special notes on care or preparation. When you're ready to use your chosen batting in a project, cut batting the same size as the prepared backing.

ASSEMBLING THE QUILT

1. Examine wrong side of quilt top closely; trim any seam allowances and clip any threads that may show through the front of the quilt. Press quilt top.
2. If quilt top is to be marked before layering, mark quilting lines (see **Marking Quilting Lines**).
3. Place backing **wrong** side up on a flat surface. Use masking tape to tape edges of backing to surface. Place batting on top of backing fabric. Smooth batting gently, being careful not to stretch or tear. Center quilt top **right** side up on batting.

4. If hand quilting, begin in the center and work toward the outer edges to hand baste all layers together. Use long stitches and place basting lines approximately 4" apart *(Fig. 26)*. Smooth fullness or wrinkles toward outer edges.

Fig. 26

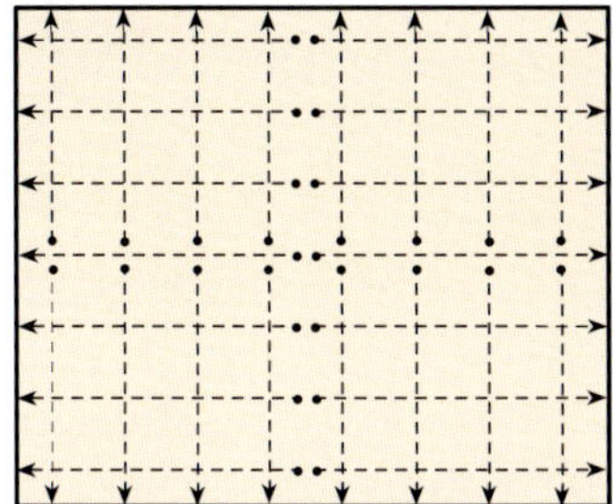

5. If machine quilting, use 1" rustproof safety pins to "pin-baste" all layers together, spacing pins approximately 4" apart. Begin at the center and work toward the outer edges to secure all layers. If possible, place pins away from areas that will be quilted, although pins may be removed as needed when quilting.

HAND QUILTING

The quilting stitch is a basic running stitch that forms a broken line on the quilt top and backing. Stitches on the quilt top and backing should be straight and equal in length.

1. Secure center of quilt in hoop or frame. Check quilt top and backing to make sure they are smooth. To help prevent puckers, always begin quilting in the center of the quilt and work toward the outside edges.
2. Thread needle with an 18" - 20" length of quilting thread; knot 1 end. Using a thimble, insert needle into quilt top and batting approximately 1/2" from where you wish to begin quilting. Bring needle up at the point where you wish to begin *(Fig. 27)*; when knot catches on quilt top, give thread a quick, short pull to "pop" knot through fabric into batting *(Fig. 28)*.

Fig. 27

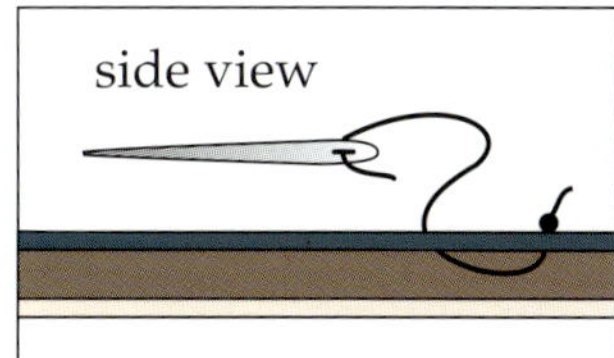

Fig. 28

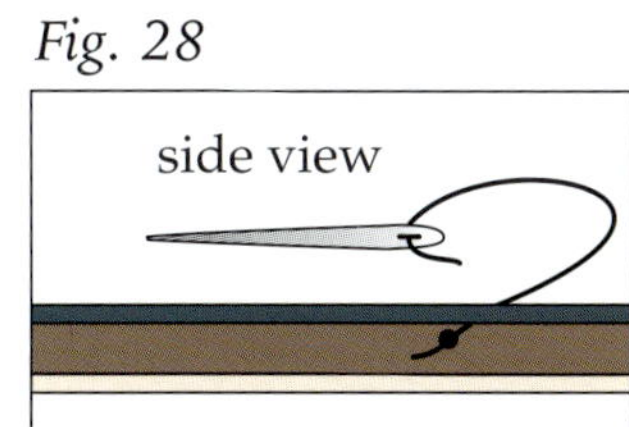

3. Holding the needle with your sewing hand and placing your other hand underneath the quilt, use thimble to push the tip of the needle down through all layers. As soon as needle touches your finger underneath, use that finger to push the tip of the needle only back up through the layers to top of quilt. (The amount of the needle showing above the fabric determines the length of the quilting stitch.) Referring to *Fig. 29*, rock the needle up and down, taking 3 - 6 stitches before bringing the needle and thread completely through the layers. Check the back of the quilt to make sure stitches are going through all layers. When quilting through a seam allowance or quilting a curve or corner, you may need to make 1 stitch at a time.

Fig. 29

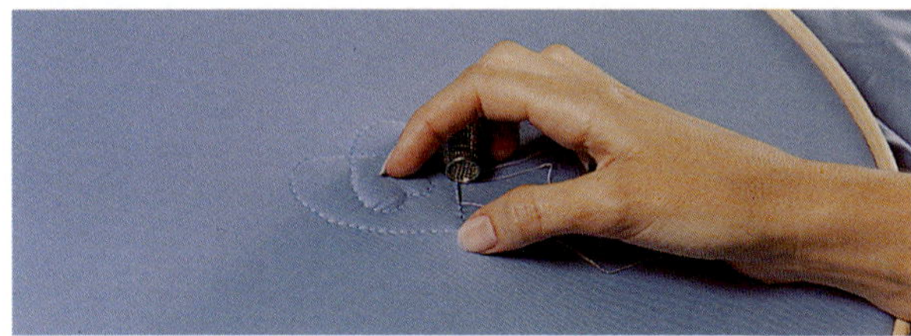

4. When you reach the end of your thread, knot thread close to the fabric and "pop" knot into batting; clip thread close to fabric.
5. Stop and move your hoop as often as necessary. You do not have to tie a knot every time you move your hoop; you may leave the thread dangling and pick it up again when you return to that part of the quilt.

MACHINE QUILTING

The following instructions are for straight-line quilting, which requires a walking foot or even-feed foot. The term "straight-line" is somewhat deceptive, since curves (especially gentle ones) as well as straight lines can be stitched with this technique.

1. Wind your sewing machine bobbin with general-purpose thread that matches the quilt backing. Do not use quilting thread. Thread the needle of your machine with transparent monofilament thread if you want your quilting to blend with your quilt top fabrics. Use decorative thread, such as a metallic or contrasting-color general-purpose thread, when you want the quilting lines to stand out more. Set the stitch length for 6 - 10 stitches per inch and attach the walking foot to sewing machine.

2. After pin-basting, decide which section of the quilt will have the longest continuous quilting line, oftentimes the area from center top to center bottom. Leaving the area exposed where you will place your first line of quilting, roll up each edge of the quilt to help reduce the bulk, keeping fabrics smooth. Smaller projects may not need to be rolled.
3. Start stitching at beginning of longest quilting line, using very short stitches for the first 1/4" to "lock" beginning of quilting line. Stitch across project, using one hand on each side of the walking foot to slightly spread the fabric and to guide the fabric through the machine. Lock stitches at end of quilting line.
4. Continue machine quilting, stitching longer quilting lines first to stabilize the quilt before moving on to other areas.

BINDING

Binding encloses the raw edges of your quilt. Because of its stretchiness, bias binding works well for binding projects with curves or rounded corners and tends to lie smooth and flat in any given circumstance. It is also more durable than other types of binding.

MAKING CONTINUOUS BIAS STRIP BINDING

Bias strips for binding can simply be cut and pieced to the desired length. However, when a long length of binding is needed, the "continuous" method is quick and accurate.

1. Cut a square from binding fabric the size indicated in the project instructions. Cut square in half diagonally to make 2 triangles.
2. With right sides together and using a 1/4" seam allowance, sew triangles together *(Fig. 30)*; press seam allowance open.

Fig. 30

3. On wrong side of fabric, draw lines the width of the binding as specified in the project instructions, usually 2 1/4" *(Fig. 31)*. Cut off any remaining fabric less than this width.

Fig. 31

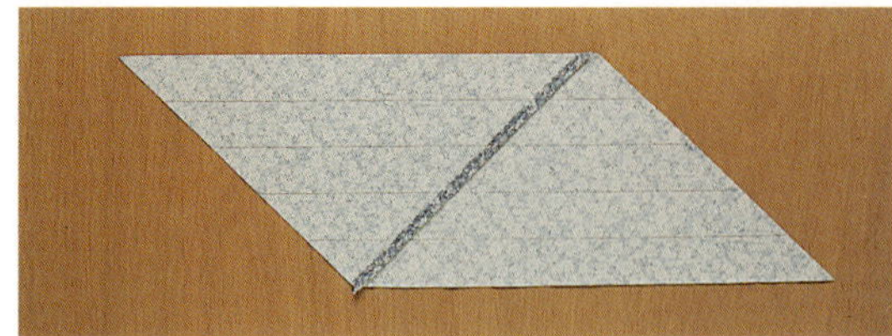

4. With right sides inside, bring short edges together to form a tube; match raw edges so that first drawn line of top section meets second drawn line of bottom section *(Fig. 32)*.

Fig. 32

5. Carefully pin edges together by inserting pins through drawn lines at the point where drawn lines intersect, making sure the pins go through intersections on both sides. Using a 1/4" seam allowance, sew edges together. Press seam allowance open.
6. To cut continuous strip, begin cutting along first drawn line *(Fig. 33)*. Continue cutting along drawn line around tube.

Fig. 33

7. Trim ends of bias strip square.

ATTACHING FRENCH-FOLD BINDING WITH MITERED CORNERS

1. Matching wrong sides and raw edges, press binding strip in half lengthwise to complete binding. Press 1 end of binding diagonally (*Fig. 34*).

Fig. 34

2. Beginning with pressed end several inches from a corner, lay binding around quilt to make sure that seams in binding will not end up at a corner. Adjust placement if necessary. Matching raw edges of binding to raw edge of quilt top, pin binding to right side of quilt along 1 edge.
3. When you reach the first corner, mark 1/4" from corner of quilt top (*Fig. 35*).

Fig. 35

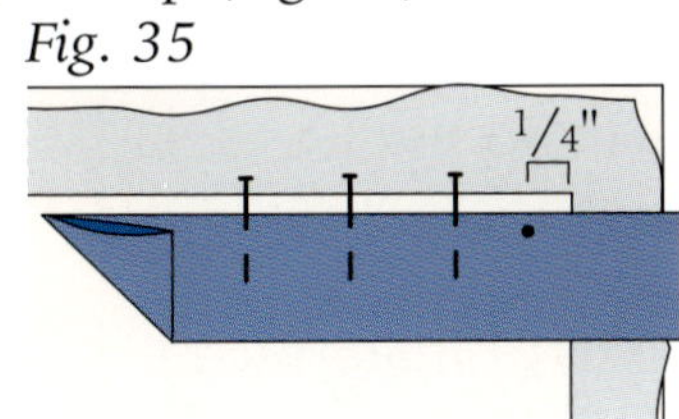

4. Using a 1/4" seam allowance, sew binding to quilt, backstitching at beginning of stitching and when you reach the mark (*Fig. 36*). Lift needle out of fabric and clip thread.

Fig. 36

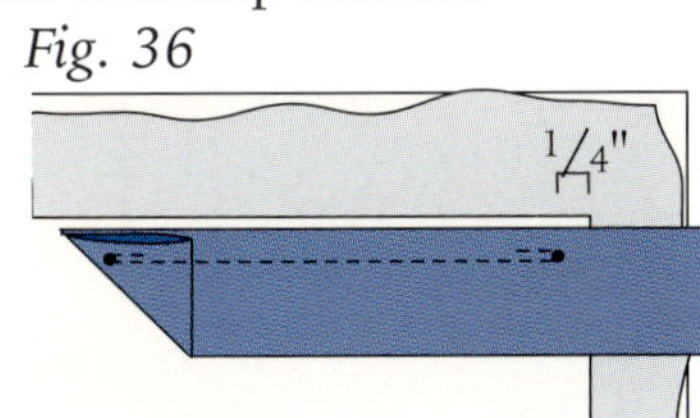

5. Fold binding as shown in *Figs. 37* and *38* and pin binding to adjacent side, matching raw edges. When you reach the next corner, mark 1/4" from edge of quilt top.

Fig. 37

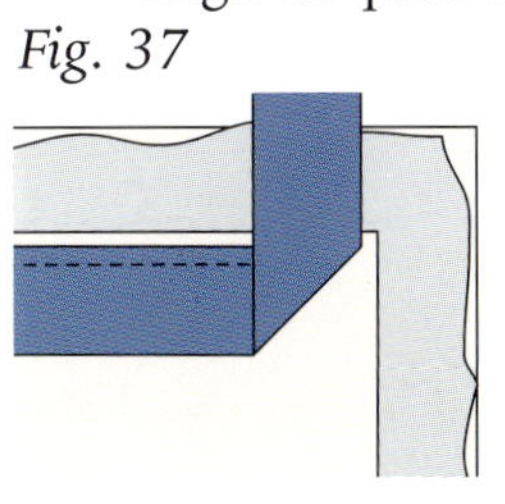

Fig. 38

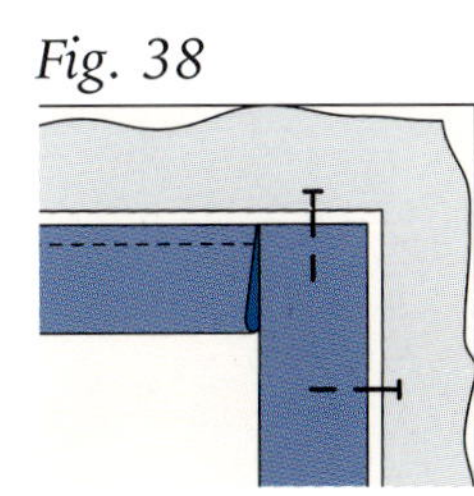

6. Backstitching at edge of quilt top, sew pinned binding to quilt (*Fig. 39*); backstitch when you reach the next mark. Lift needle out of fabric and clip thread.

Fig. 39

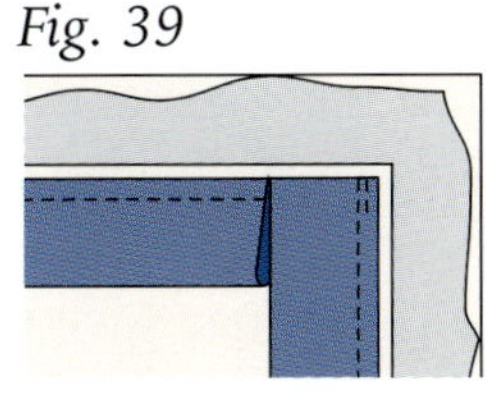

7. Repeat Steps 5 and 6 to continue sewing binding to quilt until binding overlaps beginning end by approximately 2". Trim excess binding.
8. If using 2 1/4"-wide binding (finished size 1/2"), trim backing and batting a scant 1/4" larger than quilt top so that batting and backing will fill the binding when it is folded over to the quilt backing. If using narrower binding, trim backing and batting even with edges of quilt top.
9. On 1 edge of quilt, fold binding over to quilt backing and pin pressed edge in place, covering stitching line (*Fig. 40*). On adjacent side, fold binding over, forming a mitered corner (*Fig. 41*). Repeat to pin remainder of binding in place.

Fig. 40 *Fig. 41*

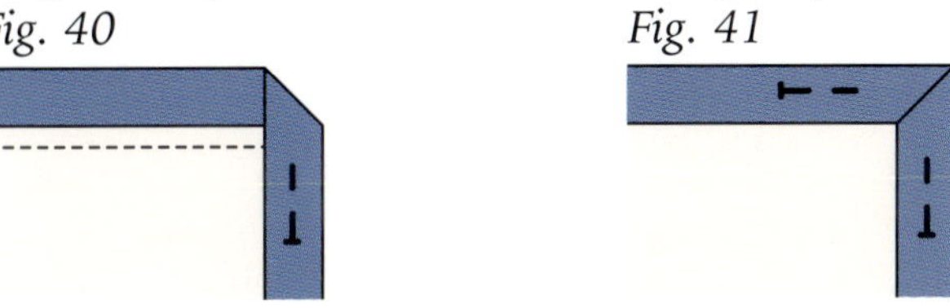

10. Blindstitch binding to backing, taking care not to stitch through to front of quilt. To make blind stitch, come up at 1. Go down at 2 and come up at 3. Length of stitches may be varied as desired.

Fig. 42

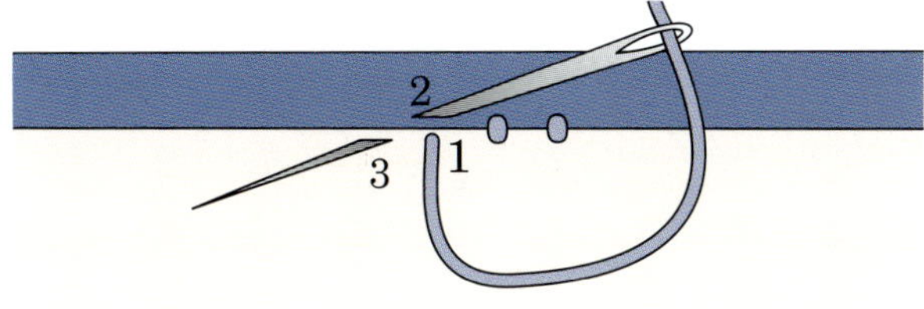

SIGNING AND DATING YOUR QUILT

Your completed quilt is a work of art and should be signed and dated. There are many different ways to do this, and you should pick a method that reflects the style of the quilt, the occasion for which it was made, and your own particular talents.

The following suggestions may give you an idea for recording the history of your quilt for future generations.

- Embroider your name, the date, and any additional information on the quilt top or backing. You may choose embroidery floss colors that closely match the fabric you are working on, such as white floss on a white border, or contrasting colors may be used.
- Make a label from muslin and use a permanent marker to write your information. Your label may be as plain or as fancy as you wish. Stitch the label to the back of the quilt.
- Chart a cross-stitch label design that includes the information you wish and stitch it in colors that complement the quilt. Stitch the finished label to the quilt backing.

Metric Conversion Chart

Inches x 2.54 = centimeters (cm)	Yards x .9144 = meters (m)
Inches x 25.4 = millimeters (mm)	Yards x 91.44 = centimeters (cm)
Inches x .0254 = meters (m)	Centimeters x .3937 = inches (")
	Meters x 1.0936 = yards (yd)

Standard Equivalents

1/8"	3.2 mm	0.32 cm	1/8 yard	11.43 cm	0.11 m
1/4"	6.35 mm	0.635 cm	1/4 yard	22.86 cm	0.23 m
3/8"	9.5 mm	0.95 cm	3/8 yard	34.29 cm	0.34 m
1/2"	12.7 mm	1.27 cm	1/2 yard	45.72 cm	0.46 m
5/8"	15.9 mm	1.59 cm	5/8 yard	57.15 cm	0.57 m
3/4"	19.1 mm	1.91 cm	3/4 yard	68.58 cm	0.69 m
7/8"	22.2 mm	2.22 cm	7/8 yard	80 cm	0.8 m
1 "	25.4 mm	2.54 cm	1 yard	91.44 cm	0.91 m